GRAMMAR IN ITS PLACE

SECOND EDITION

GRAMMAR IN ITS PLACE

Rules, skills and activities

SECOND EDITION

Rod Campbell & Graham Ryles

Copyright © Rod Campbell and Graham Ryles 2022

All rights reserved. No part of this book may be reproduced or transmitted in any form or by any means, electronic or mechanical, including photocopying, recording or by any information storage and retrieval system, without prior permission in writing from the publisher.

First published in 1996 by Oxford University Press.
This edition published in 2022 by Amba Press.

Amba Press
Melbourne, Australia
www.ambapress.com.au

Cover Designer – Tess McCabe

Printed by IngramSpark

ISBN: 9781922607287 (pbk)
ISBN: 9781922607294 (ebk)

A catalogue record for this book is available from the National Library of Australia.

CONTENTS

About the authors	vii
Introduction	ix
Part A: teaching grammar with different text types	**1**
Narrative and imaginative writing	3
Informative writing	19
Report writing	37
Review writing	59
Persuasive writing	69
Letter writing and messaging	75
Dialogue and scriptwriting	87
Diary and journal writing	97
Part B: teaching the language of grammar	**113**
Sentences	117
Phrases	121
Clauses	123
Conjunctions	135
Nouns	137
Verbs	145
Adjectives	155
Adverbs	161
Pronouns	167
Prepositions	175
Determiners	179
Teaching noun groups and expanded noun groups	183
Expectations and conventions	189
References	199
Index	201

ABOUT THE AUTHORS

Rod Campbell A.M. Ph.D. M. Ed.St. has taught in schools and universities in Australia and Asia and has co-authored and published more than 20 books in the field of literacy education and grammar instruction. He is a mentor to teachers and lead teachers in schools, and provides workshops and classroom demonstration lessons many of which are currently used to develop the teaching skills and knowledge of school teachers. Rod provides teacher professional development courses through two major teaching associations.

Graham Ryles O.A.M. M.A. M.Ed. has taught in primary and secondary schools and for many years was convenor of English for primary and secondary schools in Victoria. For many years, Graham was an executive member of the Melbourne University Galleries Society. He is now writing articles about Melbourne's history.

Their books have been published in Australia, New Guinea and Canada.

INTRODUCTION

Communication about ways in which writing ability and style are developed is easier when teachers and students have shared understandings of terms about grammar, usage, style and punctuation. *Grammar in its Place* addresses this issue using a number of questions.

- What knowledge of English do teachers need to have?
- What knowledge of English do students need to have?
- How can teachers help students learn to talk about grammar?

Grammar in its Place is designed to assist teachers with the terms used in traditional and functional grammars. Functional grammar emphasises the way in which language functions to assist meaning, but also relies upon knowledge, understanding and use of the terms of traditional grammar. The structure and content of this book is based on the following beliefs about teaching and learning of language.

In writing this book, we believe that:
- Students bring to their study of written language their implicit understanding of the nature and function of spoken English.

- Grammar can be integrated implicitly and explicitly into the classroom program into all curriculum areas.
- Knowledge of grammar is gained through classroom discussions of a variety of texts and discussions about students' writing.
- Knowledge of grammar can assist clear, concise and effective expression.
- Teachers and students need appropriate terms for talking about language.
- The language of grammar describes the functions of spoken and written English.
- Information about grammar given to students should be accurate, contain up-to-date examples, present ideas that use students' prior knowledge of language, and aim to help students become comfortable using grammar in discussion of their own and others' writing.

The teaching and learning of grammar should not be prescriptive and should not be based only upon the kinds of activities to be found in the grammar 'drill' books of the past.

There are four aims of *Version 9* of the *Australian Curriculum: English*, and this book addresses the second aim directly as well as contributing to the other three. That second aim is:

> *understand how Standard Australian English works in its spoken and written forms, and in combination with non-linguistic forms of communication, to create meaning.*

The knowledge and activities contained in this book assist teachers and students to discover and use the patterns of English, particularly written English, with a focus on types of texts and on developing student choices in the use of clauses, phrases and noun groups in sentences. The aim of the book is consistent with the curriculum in that students are encouraged and taught to understand and use a consistent language for talking about English.

The focuses of this book on *Text Structure and Organisation*, and on *Language for Expressing and Developing Ideas* make this edition of *Grammar in its Place* a helpful and practical component of teaching English.

Using this book

Part A of this book presents a variety of different text types and the grammar and linguistic features associated with each one. The grammatical features you use will vary according to the audience and the purpose for the pieces of writing.

Decide which text type you wish the students to write; e.g. a diary. You may use any number of approaches to introduce the text type or to develop further the students' understanding of its features.

The approaches:
- Demonstration: demonstrate how to write and use the text types
- Modelling: model to show the processes you are using
- Conferencing: individual students, pairs, small groups, peer conferencing
- Proofreading: individual students, pairs, small groups, teacher with small group or whole class.

Read the activities section of the text type you are using with the students. Choose the activities you wish to develop.
- Decide the format of the session; i.e. which of the approaches to use.
- Decide the size of the group.
- Follow the outline of the activity.
- Provide students with feedback and reinforcement.
- Allow students to undertake follow-up after the lesson.
- Provide further activities to give practice.
- Monitor individual student work and give feedback.

Note:
- Only use one activity at a time.
- Encourage students to use new ideas in their writing.
- Get students to record what they have learned on their Achievement Sheet, which may be titled, 'What I've learned in English in Grade Z'.
- Before working in the text type again, remind or ask students about what they have written and learned.
- Use grammatical terms with students to talk about their work.

All text types are used in other curriculum areas:
- science: explanation, procedure, factual report, description, informative, persuasive
- HASS: dialogue and script writing, report and diary, informative, persuasive
- health: report writing, informative, persuasive
- music and art knowledge: review writing, informative, persuasive
- religious education: diary and journal writing, informative, persuasive.

Part B deals with the knowledge, understandings and the terms used in traditional and functional grammar.

The students' own writing will provide teachers with the starting point for identifying the areas of grammar that they will need to develop. The teaching of these areas can be done through incidental and explicit teaching.

Read and analyse drafts of students' writing. Look for:
- increasing control of language, usage and punctuation
- variety of sentence length, types and punctuation
- attempts to choose and use more appropriate vocabulary
- development of control of the text type being used
- correct and appropriate use of the grammar of written English
- development of punctuation
- what is missing or could be improved.

Incidental teaching is used to address the needs of individual students in conference, and focuses upon a problem as it is noticed by the teacher or student. Small groups of students with similar problems are often taught aspects of grammar when the need arises in the classroom. Incidental teaching thus relies upon the teacher's knowledge of grammar, usage, style and punctuation.

The explicit teaching of grammatical structures can best be done when teachers construct lessons that provide students with a meaningful context for their learning. The purpose of the writing, the audience for whom it is intended, and the need to follow the correct grammatical structures can be developed through the use of different text types.

PART A
TEACHING GRAMMAR WITH DIFFERENT TEXT TYPES

NARRATIVE AND IMAGINATIVE WRITING

Much narrative writing is imaginative writing, and narrative becomes aligned with information when reports, retellings and recounts are written.

The common types of narrative include fiction, fantasy, myths, legends, history fiction, romance and mystery. Through narrative, students are able to use their imagination and creative ideas. This form of writing is wide enough to give full vent to stories that can be written within a web of magic, wonder or mystery. The characters and participants in fantasy can be human or animals that may possess magical powers or abilities. Participants in mystery narratives are usually human. Texts can be cumulative, sequential, reflective or discursive.

The plot of a story shows a character doing and saying things that lead to some complication and its resolution. A character's appearance, habits, activities and personality are central to the story.

The Milkmaid and her Bucket

setting	Mary the milkmaid was going to market carrying her milk in a bucket on her head.
character	As she walked along she began to think about what she would do with the money she would get for the milk. "I'll buy some
plot	hens from the farmer's wife," she said, "and they will lay eggs which I can sell to my neighbours." She walked along thinking other happy thoughts. "With the money
complication	from the eggs I'll buy myself a new dress and a new hat," she thought. "People are really going to admire me, especially the young men in the town." She tossed her head as she imagined what people would do to look at her. The bucket fell off her
sequence of action	head and milk spilt everywhere. Crying she went home to tell her mother. "Oh," said her mother "never count your chickens before they are hatched."

The writing clinic: encouraging good writing

Introduce the terms **character, setting, dialogue, plot** and **style** by focusing on specific examples. To extend students' thinking and writing, teachers need to have a purpose for a particular activity.

Answers to Brut, Gillian Rubinstein

Plot

The novel is about a dog called Caesar Brut, his owner Caspian, his sisters Spirit and Skye. Kel 'borrows' Brut who mysteriously disappears. In trying to find him the children and their parents enter a scary world.

Dialogue

Caspian: "I don't think it's fair to talk about getting rid of him, a member of the family after all."

Letter

Dear Liz,
I'm sorry that you have moved away. I want to thank you for your help in getting Brut back. You were the only one who stood up to Terry. I hope I see you one day.

Love,
Caspian

Setting

Brut under the branches of the olive tree.
Caspian's, Spirit's and Skye's house
Kel's parents' house

Style

Everyday language is used: consider the way Kel's mother talks.

Story map built up as the story develops

p. 7   Kel watching and admiring Brut. Caspian goes home without Brut.
p. 9   Brut out roaming.
p. 17 Kel rescues Brut from the rubbish bin and takes him home.
p. 22 Kel's adventures with Brut.
p. 27 The Lost Dog Notice.

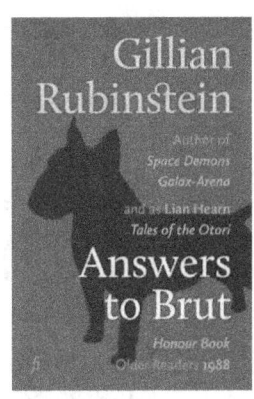

Synopsis of the next episode

Kel phones Caspian from Coober Pedy where he and his parents are living. They are prospecting for opals. Caspian is invited to stay. He plans to go but Brut disappears. Kel comes to stay to help find Brut.

Blurbs and enticers

Encourage students to write a short **blurb** for the novel at the end of the serial reading.

Space Demons is more than a computer game—it is a prototype from Japan that draws four unlikely companions into deadly struggles with a sinister force with computer intelligence. Elaine Taylor, Andrew Hayford, Ben Challis and Mario Ferrone are forced to confront the black side of themselves.
                Gillian Rubenstein

Encourage students to write an **enticer** based on the last good book they read. An enticer, like a book blurb, is meant to encourage someone to read the book. An enticer can be a series of anecdotal quotes. For example:

'*I couldn't put it down.*' Mary Smith Grade 5
'*It was real spooky.*' Tony Costa Grade 6
'*Thank goodness I wasn't Elaine.*' Paula, Riverview School

Set up a display of the blurbs and enticers near the class library.

Using a known text

Using a known text, students can see how other writers work by focusing on particular aspects; e.g. sentence expansion, story structure, sentence style, descriptive language.

Choose a known story; e.g. a folk tale, fable, legend or myth. Students retell the story using their own words. Write a class version as a wall story, leaving space under each line for innovation and expansion.

The Tortoise and the Hare

The Tortoise plodded on slowly and steadily, and when the Hare awoke from his nap he saw the Tortoise ...

As a wall story:

> *The old Tortoise had plodded*
> *on very slowly and steadily,*
> *and when the young Hare*
> *suddenly woke from his long*
> *nap he saw the Tortoise ...*

The students model stories based on those developed in class. Innovated stories can be made into picture story books and used in the class library, the school library or shared with students in other classes.

Readers' theatre

Students can prepare readers' theatre scripts from short stories, factual text or poems, which have several characters, a series of events and tell a story by using dialogue for each reader.

Red Riding Hood: An Update

Readers:	1	1st narrator	4	Red Riding Hood
	2	2nd narrator	5	Forest ranger
	3	Red Riding Hood's mother	6	Wolf

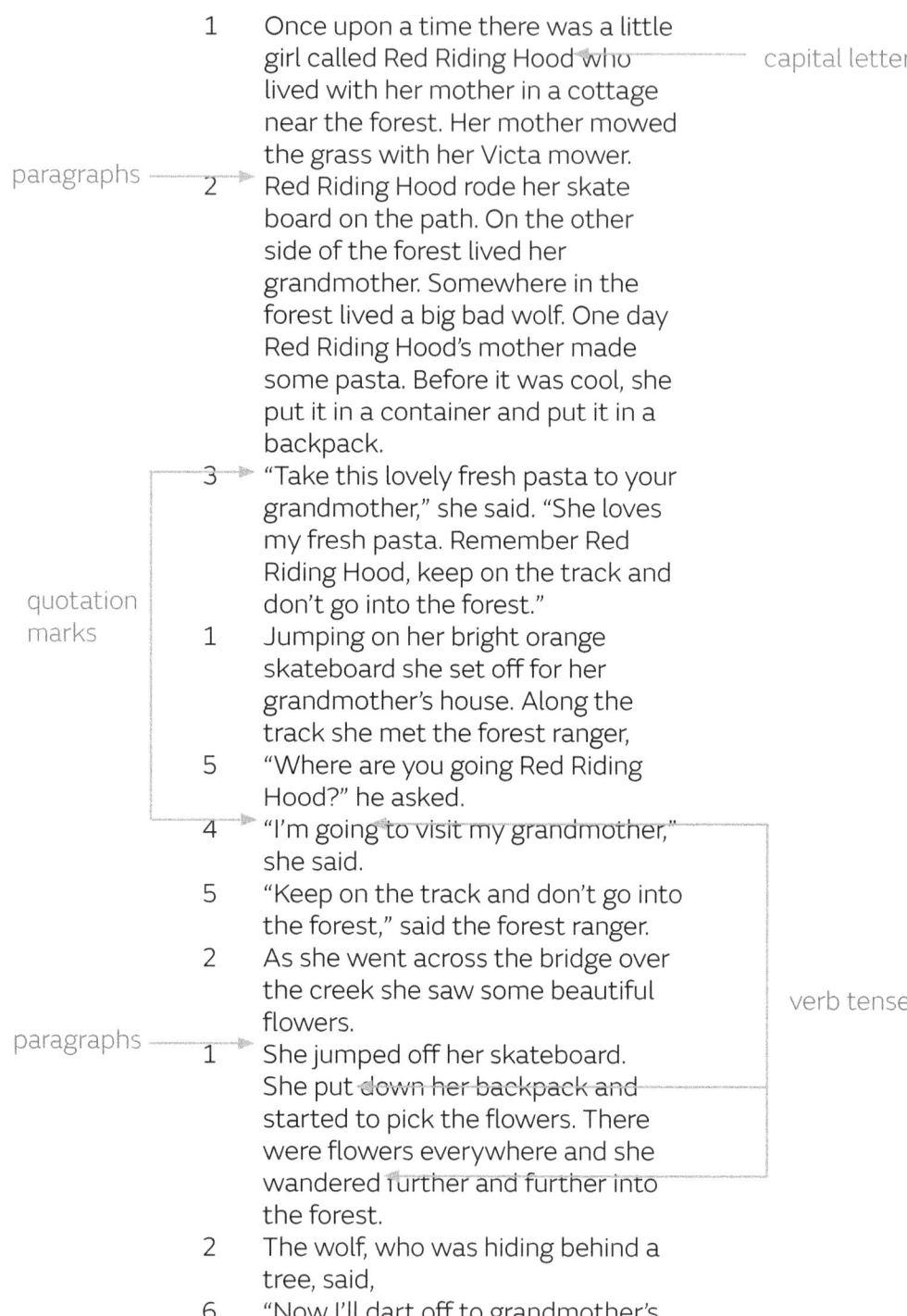

1 Once upon a time there was a little girl called Red Riding Hood who lived with her mother in a cottage near the forest. Her mother mowed the grass with her Victa mower.
2 Red Riding Hood rode her skate board on the path. On the other side of the forest lived her grandmother. Somewhere in the forest lived a big bad wolf. One day Red Riding Hood's mother made some pasta. Before it was cool, she put it in a container and put it in a backpack.
3 "Take this lovely fresh pasta to your grandmother," she said. "She loves my fresh pasta. Remember Red Riding Hood, keep on the track and don't go into the forest."
1 Jumping on her bright orange skateboard she set off for her grandmother's house. Along the track she met the forest ranger,
5 "Where are you going Red Riding Hood?" he asked.
4 "I'm going to visit my grandmother," she said.
5 "Keep on the track and don't go into the forest," said the forest ranger.
2 As she went across the bridge over the creek she saw some beautiful flowers.
1 She jumped off her skateboard. She put down her backpack and started to pick the flowers. There were flowers everywhere and she wandered further and further into the forest.
2 The wolf, who was hiding behind a tree, said,
6 "Now I'll dart off to grandmother's house and get there first."

— capital letters
paragraphs —
quotation marks
paragraphs —
verb tenses

ACTIVITIES

Cartoon strips

Collect comic and cartoon strips from newspapers. Choose four to six frames of a comic strip. White out the dialogue in the speech balloon and then enlarge the strip. Students can discuss what the story could be and suggest dialogue for the blank speech balloons.

Students can practise this task and then collect their own strips. These strips can be swapped for others to fill in. Encourage students to draw their own comic strips.

Questions questions

Use the questions Who? What? Where? When? How? Which and Why? to recall a story, plot, setting, characters and happenings. Prepare students by discussing the purpose of the questions and the style of the questions before the reading begins. *The Best-kept Secret* by Emily Rodda.

> **Where was the story set?**
> The story was set in the future.
> **How did the setting affect the story?**
> Seven years into the future the shopping centre had changed.
> **Who went with Jo?**
> Some other local people went with Jo.
> **How did you know this was not an ordinary merry-go-round?**
> The horses' painted eyes seemed to look at the crowd as if they were looking for riders.
> **What was the merry-go-round ride like?**
> It was both frightening and exciting.
> **Why do you think the riders are not allowed to remember their trip?**
> Other people would not believe them.

With practice, the students can write a paragraph to answer each question using verbs in the simple past tense.

Radio news/reports on the story

Tape radio news reports to which the students can listen. Remind students of the five 'Wh' questions, *Where? Why? When? What? Who?*, and *How?*

> Why was the report written and how?
>
> Why and how did it happen?
>
> Who was involved?
>
> What happened?
>
> When did it happen?

Where did it happen?

Why did it happen?

How did it happen?

Radio reports are written to fit a time slot.

The facts are presented in order of importance with the most important information first and the least important information last.

Students can use the five 'Wh' questions to analyse a radio news report.

Who	Five South Australian women holiday makers have been rescued from Eagle Rock off the coast of Victoria. Our reporter at the site reported that the five had crossed
Where	the shallow straits on foot at low tide to do some photography but failed to keep an eye on the tide.
How	The owner of the motel, where the women were staying, alerted police when they had not returned by 9.00 p.m. A search party was organised and the women's vehicle
When	was found in the carpark at the beach. Local police officer Jenny Long said, "It's important for holiday makers to find out the time of the tides before
Why	crossing to the island." All five are resting after a cold, wet night. Said Mary O'Connor, who was the eldest member of the party,
What	"I'll always watch the water from now on."

Students could also expand the news report into a fuller newspaper report. For example:

Who	Five women holiday makers from Glenelg in South Australia spent a cold and wet night attempting to
When	shelter on Eagle Rock, Victoria from the southern gales which swept most of coastal Victoria last night.
Where	Local police officer Jenny Long said, "It's important for holiday makers to find out the time of the tides before going out."

— adjectives
— verbs past tense
— compound sentence

Narrative and imaginative writing 11

What   Police were alerted at 9.00 p.m. by a local motel keeper that the party had not returned from a late afternoon photography excursion. "Knowing some of the women were old had me really concerned as to their welfare," said the motel owner's wife. — quotation marks/direct speech

How   "The women had gone across to the island at low tide and had not noticed the incoming tide," she said. Mary O'Connor, the oldest member of the party, said, simple "I'll always watch the water from now on." — contraction

Punctuation indicators act as boundaries and give signals to writers and speakers:

Writer signal   **full stop**: completes organisation of ideas in the sentence

Speaker signal   a **pause** between sentences following a falling intonation

Writer signal   **semicolon**: a brief pause

Speaker signal   a briefer pause between clauses

Writer signal   **colon**: something is to follow

Speaker signal   there is a brief pause following the same level of intonation

Writer signal   **comma**: indicates the parts of a sentence

Speaker signal   indicates to the speaker the possible need to pause briefly to reflect the structure of the clause complex and its parts

Writer signal	**hyphen**:	shows relationships between joined words
Speaker signal		no pause needed
Writer signal	**dash**:	a stronger indication of part of a sentence
Speaker signal		indicates a need to pause briefly or use a change in pitch
Writer signal	**question mark**:	a question is being asked
Speaker signal		rising intonation at the end of the sentence to indicate the question in most instances. (Many 'Wh' questions do not have a rising intonation.)

For example:

Making a Sale

Sales assistant:	Good afternoon. May I help you? *(rising intonation)*
Customer:	Good afternoon. You may. I'm looking for a pair of black slip-on shoes, a pair of brown sandals, red thongs and a pair of tan boots.
Sales assistant:	Certainly. What size do you take? *(falling intonation)*
Customer:	I'm not sure. Maybe it's size 10.
Sales assistant:	I'll measure your feet to make sure. Would you please take off your shoes? *(either rising or falling intonation)*

Write the dialogue for a group to read silently and aloud. Students need to follow the punctuation, using it as speaker pauses. Encourage students to read their writing drafts aloud to learn where to insert appropriate punctuation.

How will the story end?

Read or tell an unfamiliar story which has an uncertain ending, finishing before the end. Students brainstorm in groups how the story could end. The ideas do not have to be written down and could be one-line suggestions. Students can then use the group's ideas to write an ending. Individually, students can complete written stories. Encourage them to write more than one ending. Students can improvise drafted and practised oral stories for the group to finish. Sources for stories can be family anecdotes, videos, books or television and radio commercials. As students become more experienced, the story can be interrupted by students making suggestions.

A Visit to Grandfather's

Many years ago I *went* to visit my grandfather who lived a little way out of town. In those days I didn't have a car so I *had* to use the train and shank's pony. I left home early. My mother said, "*Will* you be back for dinner?" I said, "*I'll* be late as the trains are not frequent." As I *had promised* to stay with him for the day I *didn't* feel in a hurry to come back early. — future tense

The train trip was uneventful. But when I got to the station I had to get out at I *looked*, *rubbed* my eyes, and *looked* again. I *jumped* off the train. In front of me was my grandfather dressed in the strangest clothing. "Hi grandfather, where are you going dressed like that?" "My lad, you're just in time to join me," he said, "some spacemen have *invited* us to join them in their travels. *Will* you come?" — past tense / sentence simple

Thinking this was a joke for Bush Week *climbed* into the spaceship. Hold on, I thought, this IS a spaceship. Mother was right, grandfather did know some strange people. Just then two of the strangest creatures I had ever seen appeared. The door closed and the vehicle shot off like a huge rocket into the wide blue sky ... — ellipsis

14 Grammar in its place

Stories with dialogue

The Hare and the Tortoise

A <u>quick-footed</u> Hare **boasted** that he **ran** fast.
"I've never been beaten," he **said**, "when I go at my top speed. I challenge any other animal here to a race with me."
A <u>slow-moving</u> Tortoise **said** quietly, 'I accept your challenge.'
"That's a <u>good</u> joke," **laughed** the Hare. "I could dance round you all the way."
"**Don't boast** until the race is over," **warned** the Tortoise, who **looked** like a <u>slow-moving</u> stone as he **plodded** to the <u>starting</u> line.
The two contestants **lined** up and the race began. The Hare **darted** almost out of sight and then **stopped**. He **showed** his contempt for the Tortoise, **curled** up and **took** a nap.
The Tortoise **plodded** on slowly and steadily, and when the Hare **awoke** from his nap he **saw** the Tortoise just near the <u>winning</u>-post.
The Hare **ran** faster than ever before but he **did not beat** the Tortoise to the <u>finishing</u> line.
The Tortoise **said**, "Slow and steady **wins** the race."

(Words in bold show verbs in past tense; underlined words are adjectives.)

Discuss the following notes about *The Hare and the Tortoise* with students, using examples from the story.

- Narrative is often written in the past tense: *boasted, never been beaten, said, laughed, warned.*
- Dialogue is written in the present tense: *accept, wins.*
- Complex sentences are used: *Don't boast until the race is ... starting line.* (Paragraph 5)
- Compound sentences are used: *The two contestants ... a nap.* (Paragraph 6)
- Prepositions and conjunctions are used to show position, the plot and setting in time and place.

- Prepositions are used: ***to*** *the starting line,* ***at*** *my top speed,* ***with*** *me,* ***near*** *the winning-post,* ***for*** *the tortoise,* ***out*** *of sight,* ***to*** *the finishing line.*
- Conjunctions are used: ***that*** *he came from,* ***when*** *I go,* ***until*** *the race is over,* ***as*** *he plodded,* ***when*** *the Hare awoke.*

Work with students on linguistic features in *The Hare and the Tortoise*, focusing on two or three elements at a time. Choose from the list below. Remember that the most important thing is for the story to be enjoyed every time.

Points to consider:

- Different verb tenses are used: simple past tense with active voice; e.g. *darted, plodded, took, saw.* Present tense: *accept, wins, go.*
- Complex verb groups appear from time to time, particularly to note the shift from the indicative mood (e.g. *go, saw, ran, is, said*) to the modal (e.g. *could dance*) or future tense with modal (e.g. *could be going to*).
- Verb tenses may change with the introduction of dialogue.
- Adjectives providing a description are shown by using adjectives, and adjectival phrases and clauses.
- Metaphor and simile are used: *like a slow-moving stone.*
- Punctuation: dialogue has double speech marks: "*I accept your challenge."*
- Capital letters are used for proper names and sentence beginnings.

Paragraphs

Paragraphs are used to organise and structure the main ideas of information, order of speakers, introduction of new information, characters, settings and developments, new arguments and whatever else that writers use in imaginative, informative and persuasive writing.

There is no rule for paragraph length as the length of the paragraph will be determined by the writer in order to assist the reader to engage with the story, information or argument. As a general rule, very few writers now use paragraphs that are more than half a page. We know that readers are more comfortable if the print is not dense and there is a feeling of comfort from the white spaces between words and lines; and the obvious white space between paragraphs. (There are a few publishers and writers who insist on a paragraph being an indented space as the only distinction between one paragraph and the next.)

Narrative writing involves features of different types of texts. Writers will often provide paragraphs of information about background, description of settings, atmosphere and anything else needed to add detail and interest to a story. There are a number of conventions and expectations about paragraph use in narrative texts or stories, and you can be guided by the stories and chapter books you and your students are reading:

Sometimes it is useful to write paragraphs following the guidelines for information and persuasive texts. Most of the time, however, other conventions apply:

- Dialogue? New line/paragraph for each speaker.
- Introducing a character.
- Change in the development of the plot.
- Shifting or developing the mood or atmosphere further.
- Change in the development of the plot.
- Effect. (I have seen one word paragraphs.)
- Any reason the author may have.

(Remember that the word *author* is derived from the Latin word *auctor* which means the *person who started the idea*, the original source. That word *auctor* is also the derivation of the word *authority*. The author has the idea and the *authority* to control the development of the writing.)

INFORMATIVE WRITING

Informative writing, usually factual writing, is concerned with everyday happenings and experiences. Familiar forms of factual writing include explanations, descriptions, procedures, recounts and biographies.

Looking at factual writing: some points

- The **title** alerts the reader to the main content or event.
- An **introduction** is provided in the form of a **general statement** about the topic. The opening information allows the reader to enter the text quickly. It gives the reader some possibility of predicting the text that follows. The **title** also contributes to this process of positioning the reader for the information that follows.
- Further information is provided with a new **paragraph** for each major point or topic. Each new point is provided in a **topic sentence**, which is often, but not always, the first sentence in the paragraph. The rest of the paragraph consists of information and examples that illustrate the main points and the ideas presented. There is a logical progression from one paragraph to the next.

- Information is provided using the simple present tense; e.g. *love, think*. Often the verb to be is used in its simple present form; e.g. *am, is, are.*
- New points and main items of information or opinion or fact are presented so that the final paragraph provides a satisfactory **summary** or conclusion. The final paragraph may also refer to the introduction or repeat the writer's opening statement in a different way.

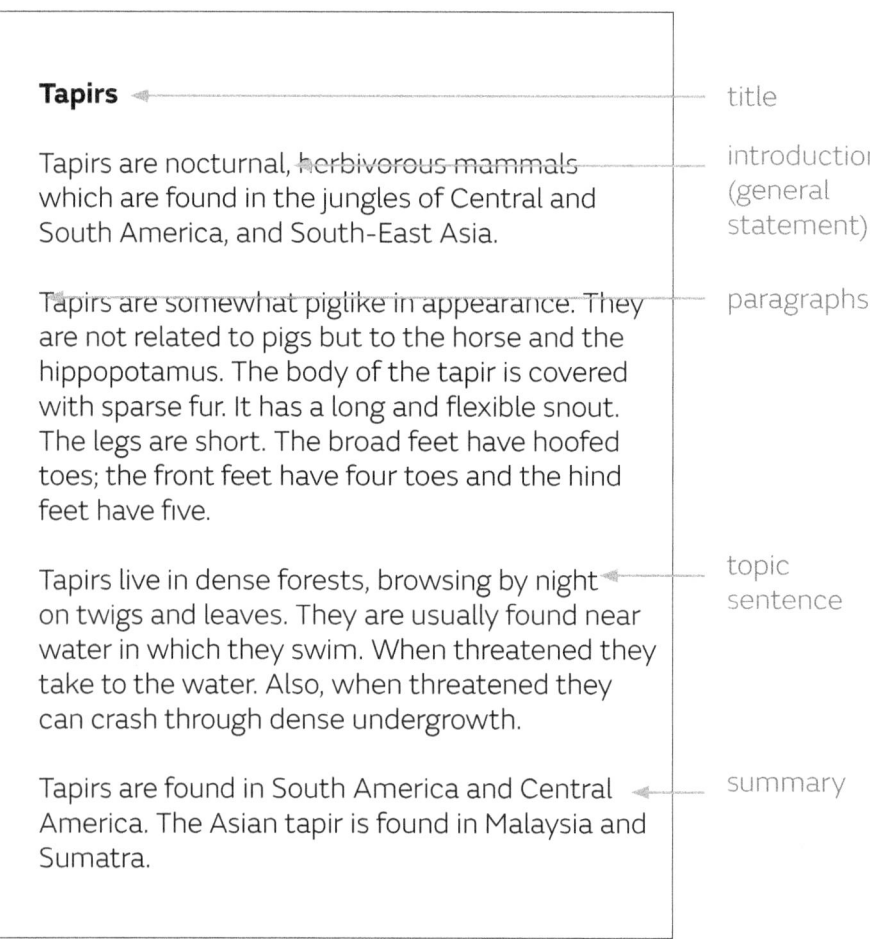

Levers

Levers are devices that people have used for thousands of years. They are used to lift loads that are too heavy for a person to lift without help. The seesaw is a lever which children use to lift each other. At the middle of the seesaw plank is the horse that acts as the fulcrum for lifting the load.

Levers need a fulcrum, and the place where the fulcrum is placed along the lever determines how useful it is (its mechanical advantage). If the fulcrum is in the middle, then effort equals load, and the mechanical advantage is one (1). This is the principle of the seesaw, with the child going down providing the effort and the other child being the load. The seesaw is an example of a first order lever.

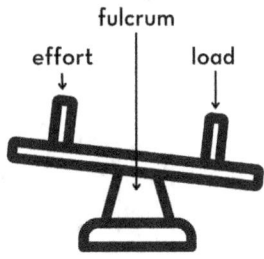

A crowbar allows its user to increase the mechanical advantage by increasing the length of the effort arm. This is an example of a second order lever. The effort required to push down on the crowbar is less than the weight of the load to be lifted at the other end.

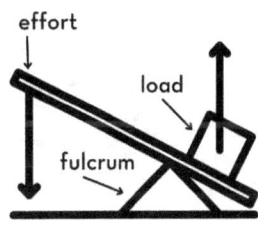

The wheelbarrow has its fulcrum placed at the end of the lever, and the load in the barrow is positioned somewhere between the fulcrum and the effort used by the person lifting. The wheelbarrow is an example of a third order lever.

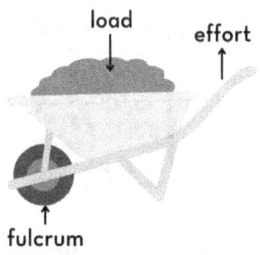

The mechanical advantage is increased with more of the load being placed closer to the front of the barrow. The greater the length of the effort arm over the load arm, the less effort is required to pick up the same load.

Informative writing **21**

Encourage students to look at a range of factual writing. Factual writing can be introduced to students as part of the school's planned writing program in all subjects. Use books and other material such as magazines, newspapers and brochures to model factual writing.

blurbs

editorials

maps

biographies

newspapers

travel brochure

timetables

menus

car manual

instruction books

questions

Why did the Americans stop their space probes?
How old is grandad?
Whom did you see at the party?
When are your holidays?

interviews

Reporter: Ms Lamma, what are your impressions of Australia?
Ms Lamma: I think it's fantastic, but I've just arrived.
Reporter: Great. How long are you staying?
Ms Lamma: I hope to be here for about a year to appear in the stage show "Red Buttons".

surveys

Fifty per cent postpone spending on new cars. Just over half of all Australians have postponed buying a new car according to Sall Poll held last week. People blamed the interest rates for their decision.

About the poll
Date 7-8 April 2022
Sample: 1000 votes
Coverage: National
Method: Telephone questions.

advertisements

science reports
Measuring Rainfall
From Monday 3 August to Friday 7 August
Grade 6 at Clifton School measured the rainfall
Procedure:
Daily Reading:
Conclusion:

social sciences
Keeping Healthy
Keeping Healthy includes good nutrition, sufficient rest, a positive outlook on life and personal cleanliness.

student recount
story writing
My Little Brother
by Allan Baillie
Vithy was separated from his brother as they fled from the Khmer Rouge. He headed for the Thai border. He met many people and had many difficulties before he was united with his brother.

personal letters
21 October 2022
Dear Tom,
I saw the film 'The Wind in the Willows'. I really enjoyed it very much. Nan is taking me to see a live production in the gardens in December.
Bye, Barbara

Different types of writing have their own structure and conventions. The purpose and the intended audience of the writing determine the most effective type of writing. Consider the following recipe for Graham's chocolate cake written as a narrative and in a procedural form. Which is the more effective way of presenting a recipe?

Graham's Chocolate Cake: The Story

Many years ago on a fine summer's morning, my mother said to me, "Graham, why don't you learn to bake a chocolate cake?" "Me make a cake?" I said. "What shall I use?" She said, "Well you'll need to get the ingredients to make it." "Let me think; you'll need: two eggs; one-and-a-half cups of self-raising flour; one cup of sugar; one cup of milk; two tablespoons of cocoa; 60 grams of softened butter; and a drop of vanilla essence."

"Next, place all the ingredients in a mixing bowl and beat at a medium speed for five minutes. Pour into a greased and lined 22 cm tin. Bake at 180°C for thirty-five to forty-five minutes."

- numerals written in full under 10
- hyphen used in numerals
- colon: indicates a list is to follow
- hyphens are used when fractions are expressed as words
- abbreviation of measure and temperature
- imperative verbs
- numbers written as numerals

Graham's Chocolate Cake: The Recipe

Ingredients
2 eggs
1 cup milk
1 1/2 cups self-raising flour
1 cup sugar
60 g softeneed butter
vanilla
2 tbsp cocoa

Method
Soften butter.
Sift raising flow into a mixing bowl.
Break in 2 eggs and add 1 cup milk.
Add all other ingredients including butter.
Beat for 5 minutes.
Bake at 180°C for about 35 to 40 minutes.
Allow to cool in tin.
Turn out onto a cooking rack.

Model examples of other types of factual writing with students. Write the narrative form on one side of a sheet of paper and the factual form on the other. Draw students' attention to the structure and the function of the text. Aspects of grammar, punctuation, style and usage can be discussed. Encourage students to practise writing in these forms.

In factual writing, apply the questions *What?* and *When?*

> *What ingredients do I need to make a cake?*
> *When I've mixed the ingredients, what do I do next?*

In writing recounts, apply the question *"What happened?"*

> *Between 1914 and 1918, a war which is known as the First World War or The Great War occurred. It involved many of the countries of Europe, Great Britain and the British Empire. It resulted in millions of people being killed or made homeless.*

In writing to tell how something works or how it worked, apply the question *How?*

> *An aneroid barometer is a chamber shaped like a very shallow, closed pillbox. The box is perfectly airtight ...*

In writing to explain or give reasons for a phenomenon, apply the question *Why?*

> *Telepathy is believed to be direct conmunication from one person's mind to another person's mind without the use of the senses.*

The 'Wh' questions are a useful focus for students in planning factual writing.

who: applies to people and sometimes animals

The children who were swimming in the surf thought that they saw a whale.
People who live in glass houses should not throw stones.
Animals who feed their young milk include horses, yaks and pigs.

where: applies to place

Where did you go for your holiday?

why: gives reasons

Why did you not come to school yesterday?

how: tells how something worked

When you place the coin in the slot, a scene appears on the screen. To activate the scene, it is necessary to follow the instructions.

what: recounts

During the football season, I went to a match between the two best teams. It was a very close match, and the winner only won by two goals.

when: applies to date, day, time, month, season, year

Winter is a good time to have a fire to sit in front of and warm your fingers at.

whom: applies to the object of a verb or preposition

This is the person about whom I was talking.
For whom are you making the cakes?

Paragraph writing

The most important feature of paragraph writing for informative and persuasive texts is the topic sentence. The rest of the paragraph usually elaborates on the topic sentence, especially reports, explanations, arguments and descriptions, all forms of writing that students will use throughout their school and university or training institution years. They will also use these skills in many careers where report writing is required.

To summarise, paragraphs group major ideas and can be structured to assist the development of the writing so as to assist the reader. Topic sentences signal and provide a framework for the development of the text and can make links between previous paragraphs. A useful framework is TEEL. (or **TEEEEEEEEL**)

T = the **Topic of the paragraph**, the subject that begins the paragraph and usually stated with a noun, or noun group, at the beginning of the topic sentence/paragraph.

Writers can select one or more of the **Es** with which to add information to the paragraph, using a carefully constructed set of simple and complex sentences and the occasional compound sentence. The **Es** of the paragraph require the writer to:

- **Expand**, **Elaborate** and/or **Explain** the topic
- Provide **Examples** and/or **Evidence** to support the topic
- Quote **Expert** opinion if credible and helpful to the information and/or argument, and
- Use **Evaluation** for comparison and support.
- Use and explore **Exaggeration** and **Emotion,** *but only in persuasive writing.* (When you see exaggeration and emotion in informative writing, the writer has moved into argument and persuasion, not just factual writing.)

L = **Link** the points or examples into the next paragraph, or to an overall theme/thesis. Use the last sentence of the paragraph to help the reader to connect or link to the next paragraph as well as build understanding of the whole text. This linking sentence is sometimes left out.

ACTIVITIES

Giving directions

Ask students to describe the route they take to get to school. Then they can sketch a quick map with street names showing their route. You can also draw a map of your route to school and model the language you use when telling someone how you come to school. In pairs, using the teacher's map, students take turns to give directions to each other explaining the route. Using their own maps as a reference, students write directions to show how they came to school.

> I come to school along Smith Street, Collingwood, turn right into Langridge Street and walk east to Cambridge Street. Then I turn into Cambridge Street, the fourth street on the right. I walk about 30 metres and the school is on the right.

My Way to School

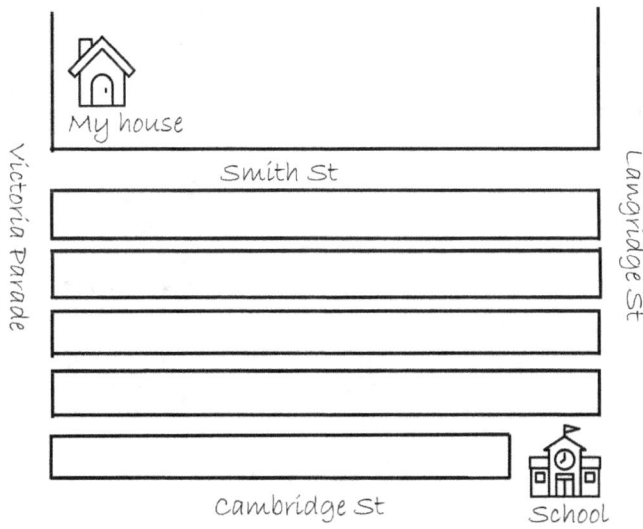

Students can use maps to show the route they take to get to sports practice or the railway stations.

Informative writing 29

Giving directions again

Encourage students to use fairytales or other well-known stories, videos, television programs or films to make maps and write instructions; e.g. *Put on your red cloak. Pick up your basket filled with goodies. Kiss your mother goodbye. Stay on the path and be careful. Turn into the woods. Pick some flowers ...* Other students can identify the original source.

Giving instructions

How to open a can of beans without spilling the contents

Model with language and actions how you open a can of beans. Try to make this humorous. Describe the likely consequences if you were not very careful. Draw and number simple sketches to show the sequence of events. In pairs, students take turns to explain the sequence used and model the language used.

1 **Take** one can of beans.

2 **Place** can on bench.

3 **Find** the can opener.

4 **Hold** the can opener in your left hand and place pointed part on rim of can.

5 **Turn** the key clockwise very slowly with your right hand. Hold the opener on to the can firmly.

6 **Click** the final section sharply and cleanly.

7 **Remove** the lid.

8 **Pour** the contents into a bowl.

9 **Wipe** up any mess.

10 **Eat** the beans.

(Note: Imperative verbs are **bold**.)

Students can then explain how to open a can of beans without spilling the contents. They can draw sketches first and label the imperative verbs. Students need to check that their draft follows a logical sequence and must describe everything that has to be done.

Students swap their work with a partner, checking the writing for logical sequence, the use of imperative verbs, and any details that may have been missed. Students can then open a can of beans or some other can with messy contents! How accurate were their descriptions?

How would you do it?

Model how you would open a parcel that has been wrapped in many sheets of paper and sealed with layers of sticky tape. Use the present participle form - *by + verb + ing*; e.g. *by breaking* each layer of sticky tape. Follow this present participle pattern with each step.

Students brainstorm and produce a list of 'How would you do it?' ideas; e.g. How would you get a cat out of the tree (without calling the fire brigade)?

Encourage students to use this pattern in their responses:

Verb: present participle form (ing): *By + verb + ing*; e.g.:

> By **getting** the ladder from the shed and **putting** it against the tree.
> By **climbing** up the ladder and **climbing** on to the branch.
> By **calling** the cat by its name.
> By **stretching** out to reach for the cat.

Students can tell each other how they would do a task by using the pattern: *by + verb + ing*.

Games need rules

Many classrooms have games with which students will be familiar, and the rules of which will be well known. Students brainstorm information about a familiar game including the size and shape of the board, the number of players, objective of the game, method of scoring, and time needed to play.

On a sheet of paper draw a table with six columns labelled like this:

May	May Not	Can	Can't	Must	Mustn't

Discuss how *may* implies possibility, *can* implies ability, and *must* implies necessity. Encourage students to complete the table.

Draughts or Checkers

May	May Not	Can	Can't	Must	Mustn't
may be played most places		can be played by children and adults	can't be played by three	must be played by two players	mustn't cheat
may be competitive				must be on a square boad divided into 64 squares	

Informative writing

Quiz time

Prepare a series of about 25 questions on current affairs, TV shows, sport, general knowledge and so on.

How Well Do You Know Australia Quiz?

1. Who is the Prime Minister of Australia?
2. Who was Ned Kelly?
3. When did Burke and Wills attempt to cross Australia?
4. How many animals are on the Australian coat of arms?
5. Where is the dog on the tucker box?
6. Why did Flinders sail around Australia?

**Interrogatives:
Who? Which?
When? What?
Why?**

**punctuation:
question mark**

**sentences: short
questions**

Students read the questions, then in pairs write down as many answers as possible. The pairs can form groups to complete the answers. Groups report back for correcting the quiz sheet.

Students devise their own quizzes using their own areas of knowledge. They will need to provide an answer sheet that is accurate.

Quizzes can be swapped and answered by others. Keep a few of the questions yourself for asking the next day to test recall.

My tastes

Students write on a sheet of paper about one thing they:

- love doing; e.g. *I love eating.* (gerund/noun)
- do not mind doing; e.g. *I don't mind running.* (gerund/noun)
- hate doing; e.g. *I hate cleaning.* (gerund/noun)

Note:

The *-ing* form of a verb can also be the name of something. The noun ending in *-ing* is also known as a gerund.

These examples use **gerunds**, which are the object of a verb. In functional grammar terms, there are two participants in the expression '**I** love **eating**.' Collect the students' sheets (without their names), then shuffle and distribute them to pairs/groups. Students take turns to read them out and see if they can identify each writer by the likes and dislikes.

Use the following example to recount some grammatical points.

Last Saturday, Dad **took** me to Lang Park to see a football game.	pronouns: first person
I **saw** the fireworks and there **was** a lot of smoke and noise. Then the teams **ran** onto the field.	
After the anthem, the referee **blew** a whistle and the game **started**. My team **scored** the first points.	compound sentences: coordinating conjunctions used
At half-time I **bought** some chips and a coke and watched the little boys play football.	
My team **played** well and **scored** two more tries and **won** the game.	time markers: temporal cohesion
After the game Dad and I **went** home and **saw** the game on TV. I **did not see** myself on TV.	

Verbs in the past tense are in bold type.

Informative writing

REPORT WRITING

Formal reports include observation and comment, investigation reports, note-taking, science reports, weather reports, newspaper reports, television reports, radio news reports, personal reports and information reports.

Reports are written objectively and are often shared with an unknown audience. Their purpose is to communicate, inform and report on events, issues and phenomena without irrelevant or subjective details. Reports are a record of observed phenomena and can be research-based. Factual information is provided about living and non-living things in an organised, concise and accurate way. Information is researched and checked from a number of sources to confirm its accuracy. Paragraphs are used to organise information. Maps, diagrams, charts and graphs are used to set out information clearly (visual language). Reference lists, bibliographies and acknowledgments can be included.

Researching for a report

Before researching a topic or subject, students need to:
- plan what they wish to know
- talk, think, read and reflect as part of the planning process
- pose the questions they wish to ask
- practise note-taking skills
- have an aim or purpose
- have a format they will follow and decide how information is to be recorded, and how observations and results are to be discussed.

While students are conducting research, you can:
- conference with students and monitor their progress in mastering research skills
- model activities to the class or group before students do them
- allow time for personal writing every day so that students can write their learning logs or recounts and complete other writing.

Classroom research area

Organise a research area in the classroom where students can plan and work. At the drafting stage encourage students to use visual language such as charts, diagrams, photos and graphs to add clarity to their writing. Use examples from published reports and books as models. Include a plentiful supply of differently-shaped and coloured papers, and different types of pens including calligraphy pens. Laptops should be available.

Interviews

Students can conduct interviews as part of their research. They will need to:
- have the purpose of the interview clearly in mind
- prepare the questions to be asked
- decide how data will be presented
- model interviews beforehand, practising being the interviewer and the interviewee

- practise the letter writing needed to organise interviews and also the follow-up thank you letters.

References

Up-to-date references are necessary for all research. Keep lists of likely sources of research material in the school, the community, the home and from businesses and agencies.

daily newspapers

scientific journals

surveys

magazines

brochures

videos

audio

Compiling a bibliography for your research

The author-date (or Harvard) system for references is used for books. It is straightforward and relatively easy to use. It is widely used in tertiary institutions.

- surname of author(s), (comma) initials (each followed by a full stop)
- year of publication (in brackets) (full stop)
- title of the book underlined if handwritten (full stop)
- place of publication whether city or state (colon)
- publisher (full stop)
- e.g. Blume, J. (1983). *Deenie*. Glasgow: Piccolo Books.

References from periodicals are recorded in this order.

- author's name or authors' names
- year of publication
- title of article
- title of periodical
- place of publication
- volume number and issue number
- page number or numbers
- e.g. Brown, C. (1992). Frogs of Victoria, *World Geographics*, Melbourne, vol. 1, no. 4, pp. 32–5.

Note-taking

Begin by modelling how to take notes. Then write the steps that need to be followed such as:

- select the material and place it in order
- look for and find connections between the facts chosen
- think about the material chosen and put into your own words.

Reporting

Students can give short oral reports on their research topic to the class or group. (This is a good opportunity to monitor the students' progress.) Class reporters can write short reports on students' research for the class or school newspaper.

Punctuation marks in report writing

Semicolon (;)

A semicolon signals to the reader that a stronger effect or contrast is required. This mark is used sparingly.

> *Some people say that football is dangerous; it need not be so.*

Colon (:)

The colon signals that a list is following.

> *In my mother's cupboard I found the following items: scissors, string, used paper, old shopping lists and a jar of dried paste.*

Brackets (parenthesis) ( )

Round brackets are used to enclose information that is not essential to a sentence but which may clarify or add meaning to the sentence. Brackets should be avoided in most writing.

> *For the picnic we went by car to Rosebud (near where Auntie used to live).*

Square brackets ([ ])

Square brackets are used to show that someone other than the writer has inserted material into the text; e.g. comments, explanations, notes and so on.

> *Her father was a successful doctor in Ballarat [Victoria] at the turn of the century.*

Dash —

The dash signals an emphasis, or an abrupt pause in a sentence.

> *As the sun set, I sat thinking of the day I bad been through — and its sadness.*

Hyphen (-)

A hyphen is used to join two or more words to show an association of ideas. There is some debate about the use of hyphens and there are few hard and fast rules. When in doubt consult your dictionary and follow its preference. If the word is not listed, decide for yourself.

Hyphens are used:

- with colours: *blue-black sky; deep-pink rose*
- with nouns of equal value: *driver-owner; girl-child*
- with compounds made up of a noun or adjective: *hard-boiled sweet; peace-keeping force*
- with numbers and fractions: *forty-five to fifty-eight; a 14-year-old boy; a six-week holiday*
- to join two or more words to make a single expression: *cut-out; north-east*
- with a prefix to avoid ambiguity: *re-form* and *reform*; *re-cover* and *recover*
- with compounds: *mother-in-law, premier-elect*
- with compound words: *gift-wrap; high-class; free-range*
- with compound words with more than one stress: *walkie-talkie; hocus-pocus*

42 Grammar in its place

- with expressions such as: *T-shirt; X-ray.*
- to join two or more words to make a common expression: *hand-to-mouth; go-ahead*
- to join a prefix to a proper noun: *pre-Keynes; anti-Freudian*
- with a distracting sequence of letters: *make-up; shake-out; go-ahead*
- with the prefix non: *non-organic*

ACTIVITIES

Reported speech (past tense)

Use newspapers or magazines to find quotes from interviews in articles. Copy the articles for use in groups. Read the articles so the meaning is clear. Use coloured pens to mark examples of reported speech in the articles. Discuss with the students which tense has been used; e.g. simple past: *declined, had.*

Focus on other tenses in sentences used:

Smith **said** a chance conversation with a club official on the teams' inability to kick goals **had prompted** his decision to play again. "Let me **say** it straight out: My aim isn't to **make** a comeback. But I'll be available as long as I'm required." A club official who **declined** to be named **said**: "I **had** not **heard** about Smith's plans." Smith **said** he **was** free from pain and now in excellent health after his two years break from playing. "I miss the game very much, I'd be **telling** a lie if I said I **wasn't.**"

past tense: said, had prompted, declined

present tense: let, isn't, am.

modal verb: I'd be

gerund: playing

Interview: may I ask a question?

Students can interview the teacher for two or three minutes in front of the group or class on a topic with which the teacher is familiar, such as hobbies or interests. The students write down in direct speech what they can remember of the interview as if they were to include it in a newspaper. Students can also be interviewed on topics and interests.

Interviewer: Paula   **Interviewee: Ms Neville**

Interviewer:	Ms Neville, what is your hobby?
Ms Neville:	I've an unusual hobby: I collect pieces of old fencing wire.
Interviewer:	That certainly is unusual. When did you collect your first piece?
Ms Neville:	When I was 12 years old I was staying with my grandparents in the country and noticed pieces of fencing wire hanging in the sheds. I asked my grandfather what they were and he explained that before modern machinery fencing wire had been handmade. I started my collection then and there.
Interviewer:	Have you brought any pieces along to show me?
Ms Neville:	I have Paula, these are very old pieces made in the USA last century. I found them on an old abandoned farm in Dakota.

sentence structure: statement and question

Direct speech

Interviewing each other

Use newspapers or magazines to find quotes from interviews in articles. Students work in pairs, interviewing each other. They will need to prepare interview questions in advance on a topical subject or event; e.g. their views on gambling.

After the interview, the interviewer writes a brief report in indirect speech, reporting what someone said. When interviews are completed, each person presents the other with the report.

> When interviewed, James said that he thought gambling was not a good thing as some people might spend all their money on the pokies or betting on horses and not look after their children.

Passive headlines to sentences

Model a series of newspaper headlines with active constructions, expanding them into passive constructions and write them in sentences.

Lightning hits golfer.	capitals and full stops
is written: A golfer **has been hit** by lightning.	verbs: passive and active voice
	past tense
	present tense

In pairs or groups, students find newspaper headlines and then expand them. The first sentences in the article will often help.

> *Jacko injured* becomes *Collingwood player Mike Jackson has been injured.*

Recalling what happened

In groups, students describe what happens in a film or video they have watched. Students can then write a brief recount.

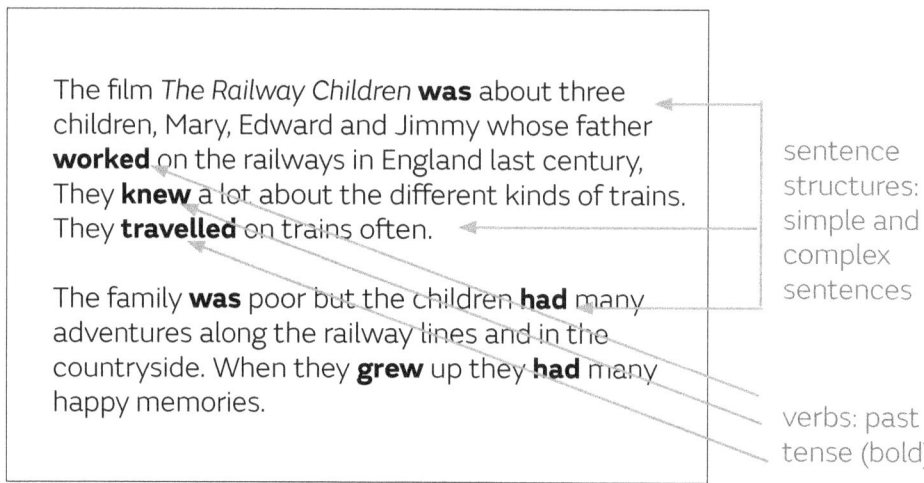

The film *The Railway Children* **was** about three children, Mary, Edward and Jimmy whose father **worked** on the railways in England last century. They **knew** a lot about the different kinds of trains. They **travelled** on trains often.

The family **was** poor but the children **had** many adventures along the railway lines and in the countryside. When they **grew** up they **had** many happy memories.

sentence structures: simple and complex sentences

verbs: past tense (bold)

Factual report analysis

Copy onto white paper a brief published factual report, or one that you, a student or both have written. Apply the five 'Wh' questions: *What? Why? Where? When?* and *Who?* to the report, and the *How?* question, if appropriate. Write down each question, leaving space between each for answers. Each group then reads the report and records the answers for each question in point form.

> **What** is being reported on?
> Australia will play New Zealand for a place in the world championships.
>
> **When** is it being played?
> The qualifying round match will be played in New Zealand from 12–15 August. — numerals written as figures
>
> **Who** is taking part?
> Australia and New Zealand are taking part.
>
> **Who** performed badly?
> Australia **performed** badly in the first round of the 2004 world competition. — verbs past
>
> **Where** did it happen? **When** did it happen?
> In April when Australia **lost** to Finland 5–1 in Helsinki.

Students write their own reports on an observation of something in the classroom, airing a shared experience on which to build. Their reports should include a paragraph for each 'Wh' question and the 'How?' question. Reports can be presented to the class.

Personal reports

Personal reports engage writers in reflective and exploratory writing about:

- their experiences, feelings, ideas and points of view
- family, self and others
- feelings and reactions, or points of view.

Personal reports are not always meant for publication or for others to read. They can be descriptive, subjective or narrative. Personal reports include personal letters, personal accounts and brief pieces of writing. They can be written in a literary style as a narrative or as poetry.

The unknown me

Students write something about themselves that others may not know; e.g. that they have skills in playing an instrument or have knowledge in a particular field.

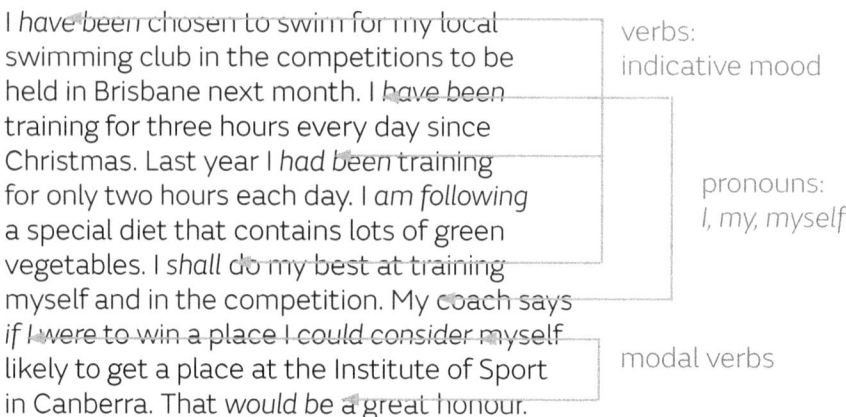

I *have been chosen* to swim for my local swimming club in the competitions to be held in Brisbane next month. I *have been* training for three hours every day since Christmas. Last year I *had been* training for only two hours each day. I *am following* a special diet that contains lots of green vegetables. I *shall do* my best at training myself and in the competition. My coach says if I *were* to win a place I *could consider* myself likely to get a place at the Institute of Sport in Canberra. That *would be* a great honour.

verbs:
indicative mood

pronouns:
I, my, myself

modal verbs

Revisiting a trip

Ask students to think of a trip or an excursion they really enjoyed. Encourage them to use sentences that follow a similar pattern to help them describe the experience clearly.

I had always …	I *had* always wanted to go to India.	verbs: past perfect
I had never …	I *had* never *been able* to save enough money.	capitals: people's names place names proper names
I had seldom …	I *had* seldom *had* the opportunity to travel anywhere.	
rarely …	I *had* rarely thought about it until one day a friend Kate said: "Like to come to India with me?" There was no holding me back.	adverb

Afterwards ...	*Afterwards* I was so concerned for the poor people that I started to give money to charity	adverb
regularly	*regularly.*	
Now ...	*Now* I have decided to return to India to help the people.	

Learning logs

Learning logs are helpful for clarifying what students have learned. They can use headings like these:

What I have learned today

What I already knew today

Three things I did well today

What I need to learn

The students can suggest their own ideas for headings.

What I have learned today

In Visual Arts today our teacher Mr O'Brien showed us how to make a monoprint using crayons. First, take a sheet of white paper about 30 cm long. Fold it in half along the horizontal. Open up the sheet on the part nearest to you and cover it very thickly with black crayon. When finished, close up the sheet. Press hard so that the two sheets stick together. Place the paper so that you will draw on the back of the sheet that has the black crayon on it. Draw a picture or portrait using a sharp black pencil. When finished, separate the sheets and you will have one print, which is called a monoprint.

Encourage students to keep updating information they have learned or acquired in a particular area.

> **What I already know about Santa Claus**
>
> Santa Claus's real name was Saint Nicholas. He was an early Christian bishop who lived in a coastal city called Myra, part of the Roman Empire. He was probably a Roman citizen who spoke Greek. He did all types of good things for people. He saved shipwrecked sailors and he saved his city from famine. Santa, however, doesn't look like a bishop dressed in his red tracksuit and funny cap.

Newspaper writing

Tabloids and broadsheets are different types of newspapers. A tabloid is half the size of a broadsheet newspaper. Traditionally, broadsheet newspapers have been seen as more serious in their reporting and presentation of the news. They have more features and in-depth articles. Newspapers follow conventions of grammar, punctuation, style and usage, making them sources of modern English in action. There may be minor 'in-house' differences. The audience for whom the paper is produced influences the types of news items, the length of the items and the vocabulary used. Look at the style of a broadsheet and tabloid newspaper and the conventions they use.

Newspapers communicate with readers through written articles and visual means, such as captions, maps, diagrams, graphs, cartoons and charts.

TABLOIDS

- present news in a concise and easy-to-read style
- use simple, common words
- present information clearly
- report items simply, with a minimum of words, and usually rely on more photographs
- may place an emphasis on violence or on human interest
- stories or sport may present stories in a more sensational way.

Tabloids contain different ways of presenting news reports: short reports, which may be a single paragraph; and lengthier factual information about newsworthy events and that range from 50 words to more than 200 words.

Different types of news found in newspapers include colour news stories, which are between hard news and feature articles and are usually of a more gentle nature; human interest stories to do with events and themes; and sporting news related to specific sporting events.

Feature pages in newspapers contain:

- letters to the editor: there is often a brief letter column, which contains many one-paragraph letters
- articles by staff reporters
- articles by guest writers, some of whom may be regular contributors
- articles printed from overseas or interstate newspapers
- a range of issues and interests
- regular feature columns
- reviews of film, art shows, theatre, recitals, concerts, arts and crafts, television.

Front page news is the most important news of the day. Headlines are written to attract the reader's attention and are often written in telegraphic language; e.g. **Pop star in scandal**.

You'll notice how newspaper reports generally answer the five 'Wh' questions (Who? What? When? Where? Why? and How?)

Gunboat diplomacy: Russian warships yesterday were stopping all Chinese oil drilling rig vessels reaching an area of the South China Sea claimed by both nations. The rising tension was not expected as both had taken part in peace talks in Washington 11 days ago. It is believed that recent oil discoveries have caused the situation.	**Who is involved?** **When did it happen?** **What happened?** **Where did it happen?** **Why did it happen?**

The facts are presented in order of importance with the most important information first and the least important information last. Outcomes are described first, followed by the context and supporting information. Reporting does not need to be in chronological order.

ACTIVITIES

Idioms

Idioms are expressions (words or phrases) whose meanings may not make sense if taken literally. Everyday English contains quite a large number of idioms, such as 'all in' (exhausted) and 'act your age' (behave as you should at your age). The sporting section of the newspaper can be a rich source of idioms, as can reported speech in news and feature stories. List idioms that students know on charts. Next to the idiom write what it means.

tit for tat   revenge

turn the other cheek   forgive

Display the charts and encourage students to keep adding to the list, using newspapers as their source.

Proper nouns have capital letters

List proper nouns the students suggest. They can use the front section of the newspaper to help them. For example, the racing section of the newspaper will contain the names of racehorses. Advertisements are also a rich source of proper nouns.

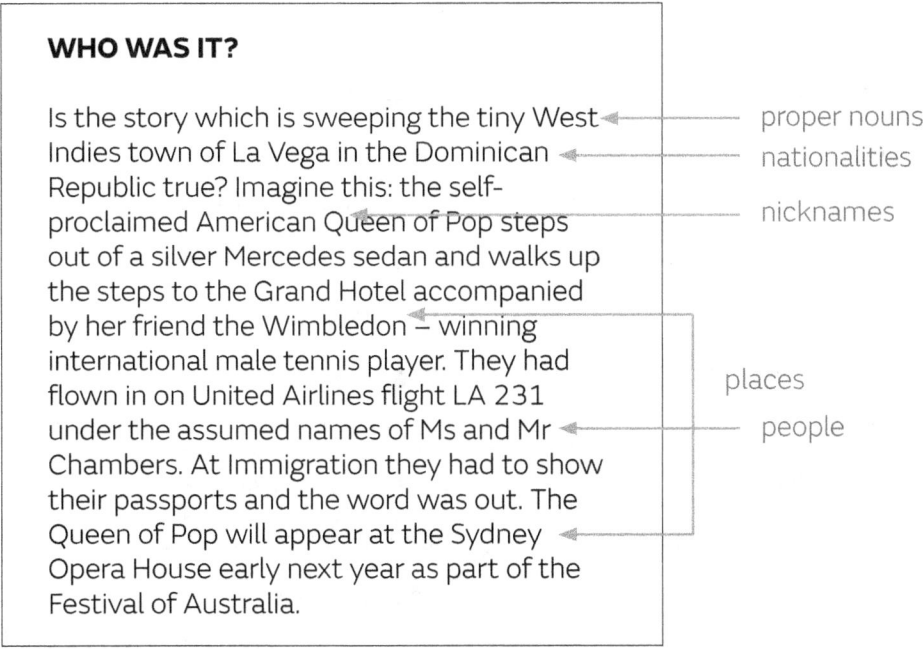

Collective nouns

Build up a list of collective nouns, *a fleet of ships, committee, crew, family, the United States, the Kremlin, parliament* and *the Senate*, to which students contribute, using the newspaper. Students' reading can also help build up lists. Keep charts of collective nouns which are treated as singular or plural; also show verb agreement.

A collective noun is one that treats a number of people or things as a single entity; e.g. *association, committee, herd*. It is often unclear whether such a noun should be singular or plural; e.g. *The crew* is/are *happy?* The answer depends on the way in which the writer or speaker regards the association or crew, on the context, and whether the group is considered as a single body or as a group of individuals.

Some collective nouns take a singular verb and others a plural verb, and some can have either a singular or plural verb.

> The public **is/are** tired of government waste.
>
> The crowd **was/were** enjoying every moment of the game.

Singular verbs	Plural verbs
the epidemic is worsening	how many sheep are really wolves?
the United States was sending	one hundred settlers are
a strange couple is at work	animal liberationists have
China has	the Eagles have
the international community is	the Olympic Games are
fruit has	oranges are
Australia was	Asian countries were
parliament was sitting	Senators were meeting
the football crowd is	the people are

Gender inclusive language

Students will continue to find sexist language in books. However, in today's society we use language that is non-sexist. English does not have specific sex-indefinite pronouns. In the past the pronouns *he, him* and *his* have been used as inclusive pronouns.

The earlier male form for occupations is used for both males and females; e.g. *author, actor, waiter, poet*. Feminine suffixes such as *-ess, -ette* and *-trix* are no longer used.

The plural pronoun *they* is often used as a singular non-sexist pronoun; *your* is also used as a non-sexist pronoun; *yourself* and *themselves* are also used. It is not a matter of singular and plural but an attempt to replace the use of *he/she*. To avoid problems, recast the sentence.

Using plurals as much as possible is best. If not, use *they* but be careful that you do not confuse your readers. For example, locate the problem in this sentence.

> *A man was injured in an accident and helped by paramedics. They were taken to the hospital.*

One is an indefinite pronoun and means people in general. If *one* is used it should be used consistently through the sentence; e.g. 'One must remember to bring one's coat next Monday.' *You* is more informal and perhaps less impersonal; e.g. 'You must remember to bring your coat next Monday.'

Tradenames, trade marks and proprietary names

Many everyday words are often generic names of the item to which they refer; e.g. *Cellophane* is a type of glossy paper, *Nugget* is shoe polish, *Hoover* is a vacuum cleaner. Such words are tradenames and should begin with a capital letter. However, many are so popular that they become common nouns and begin with a lower case letter; e.g. *biro, windcheater, thermos, plasticine*. Encourage students to look for other examples of tradenames in advertisements and news items. They can collect labels and list the words alphabetically in a class book.

Questions: interrogative

An interrogative pronoun is one which is used to ask a question. Work with students prior to the activity on the types of questions that people ask one another. Ask students to avoid questions that invite yes/no answers. Students can find pictures of people talking to one another from newspapers and magazines. Imagine one person in the picture is asking a question and the other person is answering. Students could write their direct questions as indirect questions.

Direct: Why do you have several reports to finish?

Indirect: He was asked why he had several reports to finish.

Who went with you?
Who as interrogative is used for people

How many were playing?

When did it happen to you?

Why didn't you call for help?

Where exactly did you see her?

Whose brother do you know?
Whose (possessive)

Which horse was injured?
Which as an interrogative can be used for people, animals or things

From whom did you get this?
Whom (objective case after the preposition)

What happened next?

pronouns: who, which, what are all used for people, gender and number

Which? and What? can also act as interrogative pronouns; e.g. which women? what manner?

lower case not a specific entry

numerals written as words to begin a sentence

Australians split on retaining the monarch

by Sandra Reed

Australian Affairs

Australians continue to be divided about whether we should continue with a monarch or become a republic by the year 2030. Two polls conducted recently showed a dramatic decline in the number of Australians who support the British royal family. One poll showed that 77% of Australians think there should be a referendum on the matter. Mr B. Black a spokesperson for the Monarchy Society said, 'all those who do not support Her Majesty should be put into prison.'

Buckingham Palace was not available for comment. Highlights of interviews taken on Monday night were:
- 45 per cent of those asked supported Australia becoming a republic and 43 per cent were opposed.
- 64 per cent said they wouldn't like the topic to divide the country.
- 10 per cent said Her Majesty the Queen was still No. 1.

quotation marks single

full name use initial capitals

numerals can begin sentences in list

titles begin with a capital

name of an organisation proper noun

colon used to show a list follows

number abbreviated No.

Her Majesty the Queen is always written with initial capitals

contraction

days of the week begin with a capital letter

Report writing **57**

REVIEW WRITING

Reviews are a regular feature in many newspapers and magazines. They are often written in a brief format to encourage people to gain a 'nutshell' impression of an event, a film, a video, a play, a quiz program or a book.

Review writing makes use of a wide range of easily obtained resources such as magazines, newspapers and hand-outs from cinemas. Students often enjoy review writing as it enables them to follow their own interests.

Students' review writing can include reviews of drama, quiz programs, news services, current affairs programs, children's television, TV soapies and cartoons. Review writing requires students to evaluate information, make judgments and predict outcomes.

Collect reviews of the same film by different reviewers for comparison. Do the reviewers always agree? Are there common points of agreement or disagreement? Do students agree with the reviewers?

Remind students that review writing can be influenced by factors about which the reviewer may not always be aware, such as their own feelings towards the topic, and their personal likes and dislikes.

Discuss the different genres of television and film with the students: comedy, mystery, horror, fantasy, soapies, current affairs, news, documentaries, drama, cartoons, travelogues and quizzes. List features of each genre, then categorise TV programs or films using headings, such as current affairs, soapies and quizzes. Students can collect a variety of reviews for display. Use one on a projector or smartboard to demonstrate to students how the writing is organised.

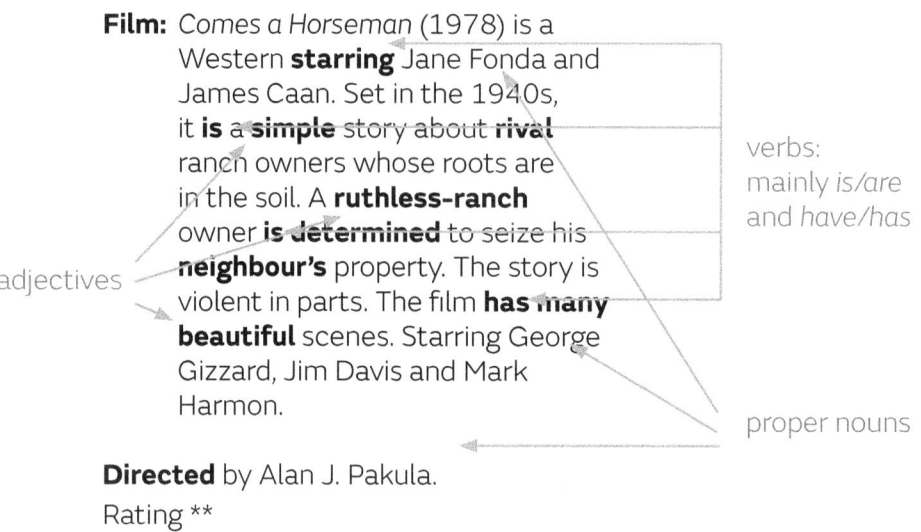

Use this sample format as a model for group writing. Students can suggest a topic and model using verbs, adjectives and conjunctions.

There are a number of conventions in review writing which are followed as they give the reader quick information. (Not all conventions have to be used.) The following information needs to be provided.

Book reviews	**Film reviews**
name of the author	name of director
publisher	producer
place of publication	writer
date	actors
names of characters	where made
summary of the plot or contents	year made
	summary of the plot or story
name of the reviewer	name of the reviewer

Devise conventions to use when reviewing videos, news reports, quizzes, cartoons and other TV programs. Develop a rating scale.

Don't bother
Maybe
Average
Worth seeing
Forget it

or A B+ C and so on

Model reviews that are chronological before the students write their own chronological review. The events of the film, video or book are dealt with in the order in which they happen.

Film: The Secret Garden

The central character is Mary, a 10-year-old English girl whose parents die. She is uprooted from Edwardian India to live with her reclusive uncle in a huge isolated house on the Yorkshire moors. She seldom sees her uncle who is mourning his dead wife. She is cared for by servants. She discovers a neglected garden and helped by Dickon, a 12-year-old nature-loving working class boy, she brings the garden back to life.

Model reviews that are a reaction to plot, character and setting, or which are a reflection on what happened and are not written in chronological order. Develop reviews that require students to make judgments about a TV program or a book.

Here is a review of a film, *Getting Even With Dad* (note the use of verbs past tense).

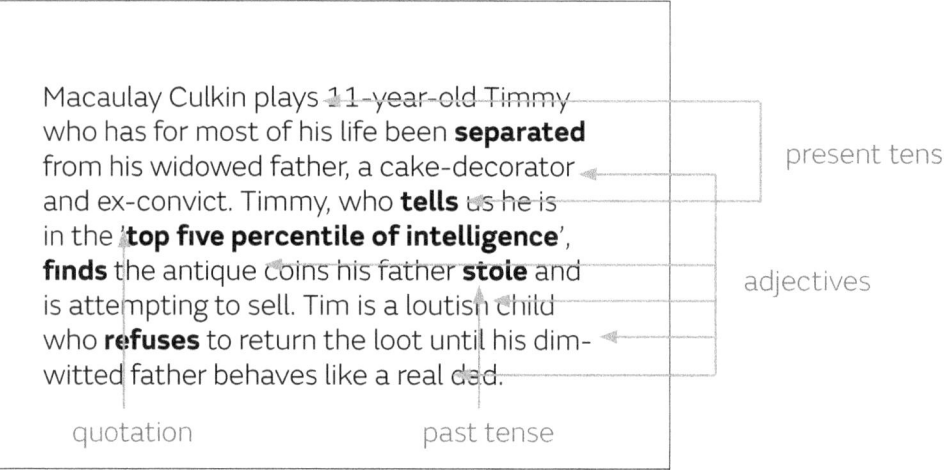

Model a TV current affairs program. Consider questions like the following: Does the reporting seem fair? How does the interviewer conduct the interview; e.g. does the interviewer talk all the time or interrupt? Is the interview being shown live? Has it been edited?

Students decide the conventions to be used to write their own reviews of TV current affairs programs. They can summarise their reviews in a sentence or two. Display students' reviews.

> *Four Corners* this week looked at the suffering of the thousands of refugees in Europe. It discussed the need for Australia to give more aid.

Reviewing school events

Students can write reviews of activities around the school.

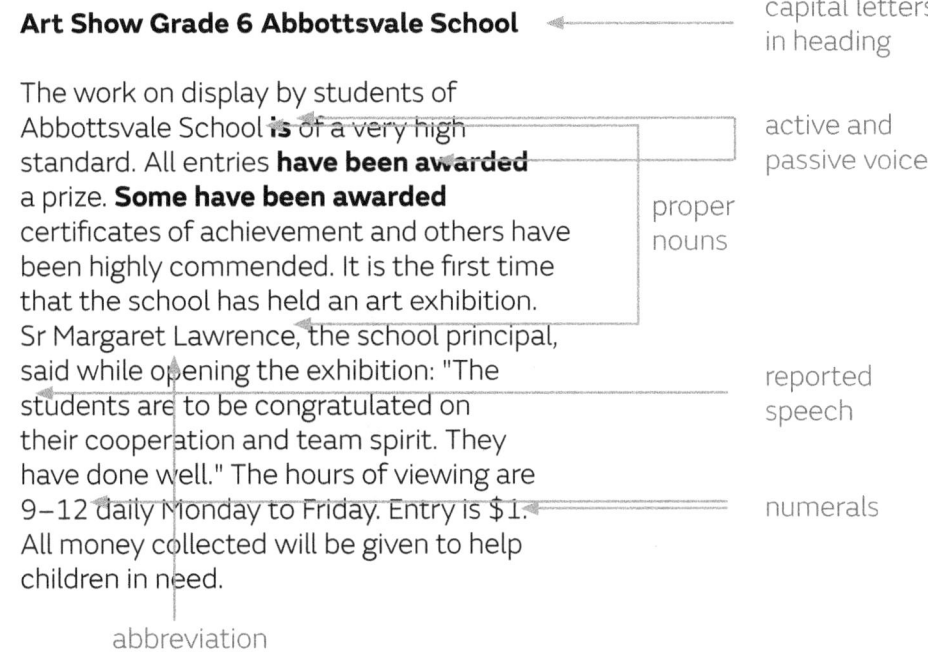

ACTIVITIES

What is the person doing?

Mime actions to students and have them guess what you are doing. Write their answers on the board using the active voice; e.g. '*cuts*' or '*is cutting*'. Students take turns in pairs to mime to each other. Students give their answers orally or in writing. List their sentences; e.g. *Marcus is walking, Jade is climbing, Clare in crying.* Ask students who is the 'doer' of the action in each sentence. Underline the 'doer' and explain to the students that the term for 'doer' used in grammar is the **subject**. Label the 'doer' as the subject.

When the subject is the 'doer' of the action, a verb in the active voice used.

> Nadal **served** well, but Federer gave the better return.

Students write a paragraph using the active voice telling what another student did.

> Pam **took** the role of a circus star and **was showing** us her newly learnt skills.

> The footballer is running with the ball. He's in front of the goal bouncing the ball. Another player is racing up behind him. It's over. He's kicking the ball. It's a big one. It's a goal. He is showing great form this season.

(and is bouncing)
continuous present tense
(he is kicking)

pronoun   contraction

What are they doing?

Follow the procedure as in 'What is the person doing?' Two students perform the action. (Give students time to practise.) As students perform their action, other students have to guess what action is being performed. List their suggestions: *are running, are walking* and so on. Then write the verbs in sentences.

> *Carla and Julian* **are hopping.**

> *Pat and Mick* **are skipping.**

Ask the students to say who the 'doers' are in each sentence. Underline the doer.

Show students how to write the sentences in another form of active voice.

> *Carla and Julian* **have been hopping***. Pat and Mick* **have been skipping***.*

Draw students' attention to the plural subject (*Carla and Julian*) and the plural verb form (*have been*). Students write a paragraph using plural subject and plural verbs to tell what action a pair of students performed.

---

singular:
was showing
has been showing
is taking

plural:
were showing
have been showing
are taking

Paul and Magda have been performing for us. They were showing us some tricks before singing a number of really funny songs. They were going to perform some more tricks but they ran out of time.

Quiz shows

Discuss generally what students know about TV quiz programs. Students watch some TV quiz programs in preparation for writing a review. Consider the following sample format for writing a review.

Name of the quiz? Wheel of Fortune
Hosted by (compere)? John Burgess
Names of contestants?
Shown on which channel? Channel 7 (Melbourne)
Day, date and time of viewing? Daily Monday to Friday 5.30 p.m.
What are the prizes?
What is the quiz and how do you win or lose? (in a paragraph)
What kinds of commercials are shown and how often?
What is the intended audience? (The types of commercials will help you with this: gender, age, location and so on.)
Review paragraph of viewers' responses

Students can use this format or one devised by the class. Students present their reviews to another student who has watched the same quiz. They need to check reviews for accuracy.

Other television reviews

Model formats to review other types of TV programs. Students watch more than one channel on more than one occasion. The name of the program, the channel and the time is to be recorded.

News programs: What items of news come first/last? How much time is devoted to foreign, national and local news? Are all types of people shown?

> **Name of news program: News, Sport, Weather. Channel 6. Time: 6.00 p.m.**
>
> The first item in tonight's news was the crisis in the Ukraine. It was followed by the Peace Talks in Paris. After the first commercial (expensive 4-wheel drive car), the news was from Canberra where the prime minister was interviewed by Sally Catkin about feral animals …

Sports programs: What kind of sports are shown? What kind of sports are not shown? Are women's sports shown? Are sports people with disabilities shown?

Serials: Who are the characters? What is the setting? What is the plot Who is the audience? Are contentious issues such as drug taking raised?

Soapies: Who watches them? Give a synopsis of the plot of a soapie.

Children's programs: What time of day are they shown? (a.m/p.m.) What is their country of origin? What are they about? Who are the characters?

Cartoons: When are they shown? Are they Australian produced? Who are the characters? Is there violence? Are they good for children to watch?

Film reviews

Students can write film reviews for a variety of audiences including other students in their class, for other classes and parents. The style of review does not have to be complicated. Give the students a form to model initially; later each student may develop a personal style. Students may write their reviews in a few sentences.

As most students watch TV, writing reviews of films on TV is probably the easiest. TV guides give information about the film. Encourage students to write reviews on the same film. The results can be entered on a grid with an averaged rating.

Film viewing

Week ending 10/11/2022

	Maryanne	Anna	Joel		Average
Enchanted	A	C	A		B+
The Call of the Wild	C	C	C		C
Summer's Out					
Frozen					

Book reviews

Book reviews can be a sure way of turning students away from any form of reading. Use them with care and vary the format used. Book reviews can include the following (*Answers to Brut* by Gillian Rubinstein is the source of the examples):

- Review the synopsis of the story so far, or of a chapter, or the entire story.

> Chapter 1:
>
> Kel 'borrows' a bull terrier called Brut. Brut's owner was looking for him but Brut did not let on where he was.

- Review the story form:

> A realistic story in which children and their families fear violence.

- Review the literary focus of the story.

> In this story the main characters are Caspian, Kel and their families. The animal Brut has the main role in the story. The setting includes Kel's home, Caspian's home and the shadowy warehouse.

This activity can also be done using the plot as a focus.

PERSUASIVE WRITING

Persuasive writing is all about making your point, selling your idea, contributing to debate, winning your argument. Good persuasive writing builds on knowledge and use of paragraphs and vocabulary, and on careful choice in types of sentences. In classical rhetoric or debate, the five principles of debate or argument are:

- inventing your argument with useful information
- structuring your argument (the rhetoric) with paragraphs and sentences
- using figurative and emotive language
- delivery of the argument
- memory (debate is a spoken activity).

Persuasive writing is similar to informative writing, but has imagination, figurative language, modal language and emotive language selectively used for effect. To state it again, the aim is always to sell your idea and win your argument, to persuade others to your way of thinking and belief.

The difference from informative writing begins in the introduction, the opening paragraph where you state your thesis (what you are arguing) clearly and then provide a list of reasons to support your thesis. Each of those reasons becomes the topic sentence for each paragraph.

Each paragraph can make use of all nine of the Es of paragraph development beyond the topic sentence.

The final paragraph acts to signal, sum up the main points of your thesis and leave the listeners or readers with something to remember. Some years ago, a group of children helped me to organise the concluding paragraph as having three Ss: Signal, Summary and Slogan. For example:

> *In the final analysis (**signal**), using a handheld device while driving or riding is more than dangerous behaviour, being distracted and selfishness (**summary**). It is a matter of life and death (**slogan**).*

Language features (rhetorical devices) of persuasive texts

Emotive language is used to try and involve the audience and readers. Often the first person (I, we) is used together with the second person (you).

Exaggerated language is used such as *Failure to heed this warning will result in terrible catastrophe.*

Figurative language, particularly simile and metaphor, is used to support points made; e.g. *The opposite to doing something to improve the situation is to do nothing, like watching a house burn down when there are water trucks ready to put out a fire.*

Parallelisms are used carefully to sell the idea, in sets of three words, phrases, or clauses; e.g.
- *This product meets all requirements for the enthusiastic gardener: safe, productive and wholesome.*
- *Saving the planet from asteroids must begin from this minute, with every facility, and for planet survival.*

- *The settlers decided to shift their colony when the tides regularly inundated their camp, when little fresh water was available, and when an explorer found better land further up the river.*

The use of alliteration in parallelisms is a regular feature of advertising; e.g.
- *Attend our gym for a physique that is trim, taut and terrific.*

ACTIVITIES

1. Students write a letter to the local newspaper seeking an interviewer to advertise the school fete.

2. Students write a letter to the local member of parliament, pointing out the value of the playground and waterway near a planned new road or housing development.

3. Students are grouped in threes and are asked to make notes for the development of an argument about the following topics:
    - Students must keep their school clean and tidy
    - Homework is important and necessary
    - Dogs make better pets than cats
    - Sporting personalities are paid too much
    - Cricket is the best game ever
    - Climate change is the greatest danger to existence
    - (...my favourite holiday place...) is the best place on earth.

Model the process with the students on the smartboard or whiteboard or on their tablets, and make use of their contributions so that they know how to organise the opening paragraph and the topics for the following paragraphs. (Note: Students will also need lessons and activities in summarising information in order to bring more effective writing to the concluding paragraph.)

For example:

Students keep schools clean because:
- Paper and litter looks awful, unsightly, messy, terrible
- Food scraps attract vermin like rats and insects and some birds
- Dirty playgrounds and rooms can make people sick
- Visitors like to see clean spaces and rooms
- Rubbish can be carried away by wind
- Rubbish can be washed away in heavy storms and pollute nearby creeks
- Contributing to a clean school gives a sense of pride and ownership.

Students help when they keep their school environment tidy.

thesis → Students can do great things for their environment, starting in their own school environment. Some people say that students should not pick up papers and rubbish left by other students, but the school grounds belong to everybody. Paper, ← problem stated
rubbish and litter make a place look terrible and — reason 1
uncared for, attract unwanted vermin and animals, ← reason 2
and contribute to pollution in surrounding areas. ← reason 3
As well, working together on an ongoing and
necessary project builds consistency and pride in ← reason 4
the community of students.

topic sentence → Visitors gain a positive impression of a school when they see an area that is clean and cared for. Papers moving around the grounds with the breeze, and
imagery → little piles of discarded food make most people uncomfortable. Parents may choose to avoid sending their children to a place that looks untidy, — parallelism (with alliteration)
unsafe and unedifying. ←

Vermin such as rats and cockroaches thrive in — emotive
places where rotting food has been left for days. — language
appeal → Wonderful Australian birds such crows and ibises
to helping learn that it is easier to pick at poorly closed
fauna bins rather than find their food in their natural

72 Grammar in its place

environment. People do not have a good opinion of bin chickens that scavenge among the mess that people themselves can create in school grounds. — emotive language

topic sentence → Paper and plastic items are blown away by the wind and washed away from school grounds into drains that flow into and pollute local creeks. This pollution causes trouble for the animals and plants that rely upon unpolluted waterways and creekbanks and parks. And such rubbish looks bad whether it is in the schoolground or nearby areas. — comparison

summary signal → In summary, there are two solutions to the problem ← top level structure of litter. The first is to have no rubbish to throw away, but that is not entirely possible. The second is for students to look after themselves and their

three reasons listed in parallelism → schoolgrounds by keeping the places tidy so that — to help summary unsightly, verminous and polluting materials are discarded into secure rubbish bins. Everyone benefits when everyone helps. ← slogan (links to reason 4 earlier)

Advertising

Advertising is a special kind of persuasive writing, and modern advertising uses pictures, colour, movies and all sorts of visual methods to add to spoken and written language. The purpose is to convince people to spend their money on a preferred product, vote for someone or change their lifestyle. We live with advertising every day. All of the information about persuasive writing can be used in advertising, but with the necessary qualification that the message needs to be short and to the point.

ACTIVITIES

1. Write an advertisement to sell your unwanted bicycle or skateboard.

2. Develop a brochure to advertise your suburb or town. Use an A4 sheet of paper and fold into three (DL style), giving six spaces for setting out information and illustrations. For example:

Fold into three

Outside

front	fold	back
Name of suburb and photo	Good things about your town	Contact persons – Shire Office, Town Council etc.

Inside

left	middle	right
Buildings and businesses	Parks, rivers and tourist attractions	Recreation attractions

LETTER WRITING and MESSAGING

The advent of computers and mobile phones has lessened the use of letter writing and other forms of traditional writing. Yet many of the earlier conventions still apply. There are two main types of letter writing: formal business letters, which are more precise, and less formal personal letters. Personal letters include invitations and acceptances, which have set formats, and other letters that are not formal and can be chatty, long or short, and range over a number of topics (greetings, best wishes, compliments, informal letters, notes).

Business letters include orders for goods, applying for jobs, requests for information, letters of complaint, letters of suggestion and letters to the editor of a newspaper. Such letters are concise, accurate and provide all the necessary information concerning one, two or more matters.

What are the conventions?

Letter writing involves conventions that must be taught and closely followed by students. These conventions include:

- setting out letters with appropriate salutation and closure
- using correct punctuation
- addressing an envelope correctly
- using a writing style that is appropriate for the purpose and audience of the letter
- using contractions, abbreviations and paragraphs correctly

Business letters are usually written using open punctuation.

Example of a business letter

12 April 2022	the date
Mr F Brown Proprietor Happy Pets Shop 24 Tower Street Villewood NSW 2987	no punctuation is used in the date, the addresses, the greeting or the closure
Dear Mr Brown	the greeting (salutation is written on the left-hand side
Thank you for the excellent help that you gave my daughter Amanda yesterday when she called in to ask about the care of rabbits. The assistants in other pet stores are often rude and unhelpful to young customers who wish to talk about pets rather than buy them.	
Yours sincerely	a business letter closure sign your name here
Ms A Wolf 6 Railway Place Villewood NSW 2987	put your name and address here

The format and conventions of business letters are now often followed in letter writing. However, in handwritten personal letters older styles of format will continue to be used for some time by many people. Calligraphy skills can be developed for writing invitations, acceptances, greetings and for writing personal letters to friends and relatives. Encourage students to develop personal styles appropriate for handwritten or printed letters.

Word processors are now used for personal letters; use open punctuation.

Example of a personal letter using open punctuation

Letter writing is part of the English language curriculum that is often neglected or hastily taught. Letter writing is still an important way of communicating and will continue to be so in the 21st century. Letter writing should not be treated as a one-off area of work but as a form of writing that needs to be mastered. You could greet your students each term with a letter or postcard you have written — the students can write replies.

Model the different types of letter writing: invitations, acceptances, greetings, best wishes, compliments, informal letters, notes, orders for goods, applications for jobs, requests for information, letters of complaint, letters of suggestion, and letters to the editor of a newspaper.

Drafting is part of the craft of all writing. While writing, encourage students to ask questions such as: What would the writer write about? What would be of interest to others? Why would the writer be writing? and so on. This will help to give purpose to students' writing. They need a purpose for writing and could, for example, find pen pals in Australia or overseas.

Set up a classroom letter writing area which has:
- different types of pens: thick, thin, ink-based, spirit-based, ballpoints
- a selection of differently-coloured and differently-shaped papers and envelopes
- supplies of pro forma postcards
- word checkers
- telephone books, dictionaries, thesaurus and a postcode book
- examples of letters displayed for students to model. (These could be kept in a folder with plastic inserts.)
- Australia Post information on addressing letters
- template shapes (commercial cards or ads in magazines) to be used for cutting shape; e.g. of cats, cars, spaceships, flowers
- lists of abbreviations and contractions found in students' reading and writing; e.g. Mon., Tue., Jan., Feb., I'll, they're.

To encourage letter writing, provide a classroom letterbox. Establish the rules with the students about who opens the box and when, and how letters are delivered. Dress up your letterbox to make it a continuing focal point during the year by using foam or cardboard cut-outs for special events; e.g. Christmas, Easter, Book Week, Halloween and other festivals. Students could investigate books of letters by famous people in the school and local library.

ACTIVITIES

Formal invitations

Discuss with students the types of functions to which they or their parents may have been invited. List on a whiteboard how they were invited. You may need to recount your own experiences of being invited to functions with a written invitation.

A formal invitation

> *Marcia Conte has much pleasure in inviting James Brown and friend to her 21st Birthday Party to be held at The Tudors Reception House on Friday 12 June 1996 at 8.00 p.m.*
>
> *RSVP 1 June 2022*
> *1 Elm Street,*
> *Ridgeview 0011*

one paragraph

conventional punctuation

Letter writing and messaging **79**

A formal reply

> James Brown and Mary Otto have much pleasure in accepting your invitation to attend your 21st Birthday at The Tudors Reception House on Friday 12 June 2022 at 8.00 p.m.
>
> 25 Riverside Place,
> Placewood SA 8888

**abbreviations/
contractions
not used**

RSVP is the only shortened form of a word (or acronym) used in a formal invitation. It is French for *repondez s'il vous plait,* which means 'please reply'.

An informal invitation

> 24 May 2022
>
> Dear James
>
> I am having a 21st Birthday at The Tudors Reception House on Friday 12 June 2022 at 8.00 p.m. and I would like to invite you and a friend.
>
> Please let me know by 1 June.
>
> Sincerely
> Marcia Conte

**punctuation
open style**

**structure not
formal**

**more than one
sentence may
be used**

An informal acceptance

> 29 May 2022
>
> Dear Marcia
>
> Thanks for your invitation. My friend and I will see you on 12 June and look forward to a great night.
>
> Regards
> James
>
> 25 Riverside Place
> Placewood SA 8888

Writing personal letters

Encourage students to write a wide variety of letters, including written invitations. Students will need to determine whether conventional or open punctuation is to be used.

Students can write letters to other classes congratulating them on sporting, school or personal achievements, or inviting them to class activities.

Example of a personal letter using conventional punctuation with address on the left-hand side (compare this with the letter on page 77).

Writing business letters

Model how to write business letters to order goods, complain, pay compliments, apply for a position and so on. Business letters provide an opportunity for real writing. Letters to the editor of a newspaper and to government departments are not strictly business letters but are written in a business (formal) format. Collect business letters that you receive. Encourage students to bring their own samples of letters from home. Examine the style, language, purpose and audience of these letters. Arrange the letters into categories according to their subject matter; e.g. advertising. Students can write their own examples of each type of letter and label the parts.

Example of a business letter about damaged goods

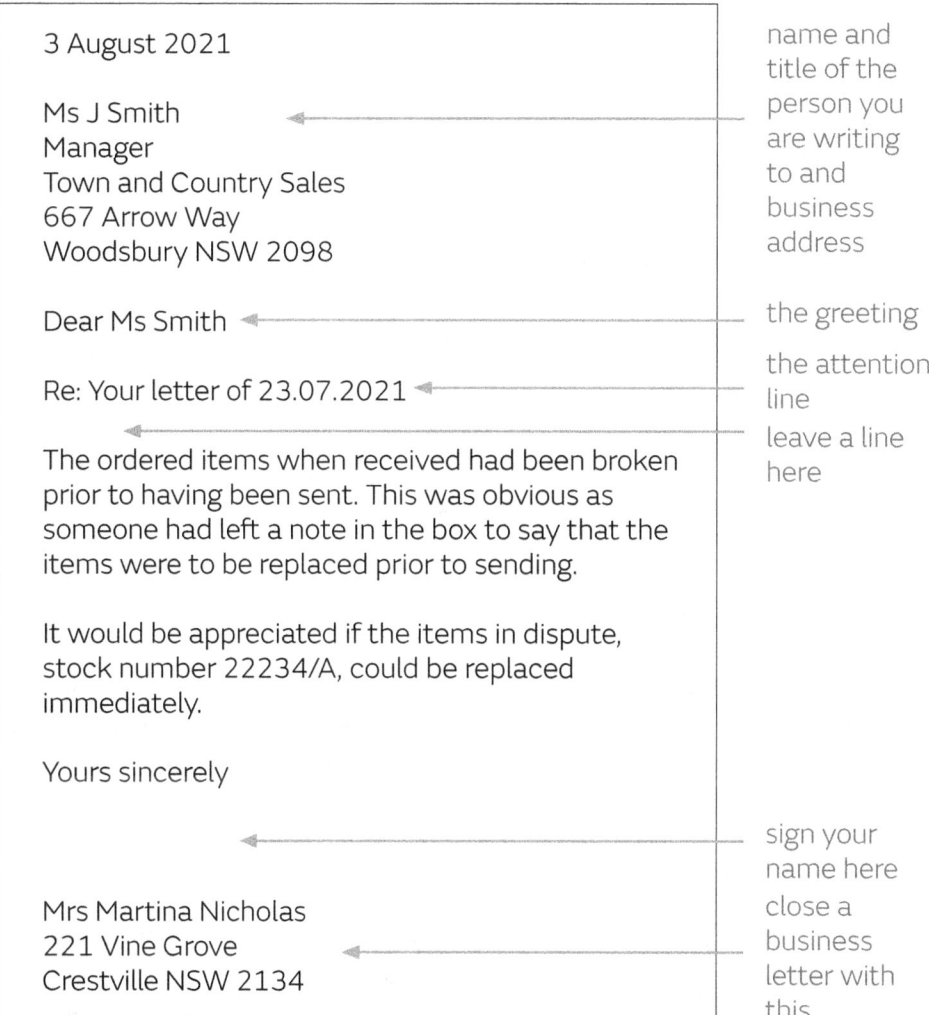

Attention line

Re is used when there has been previous correspondence on the matter; e.g. Re: Your letter of 19 January 2021. *Re* means 'about' or 'concerning'.

Starting a letter

Decide the purpose of the letter and to whom it is going to be sent. Model how to start formal and informal letters. Students choose the purpose of the letter and to whom they are going to write. They will need to determine how formal it will be. Build up charts showing examples of letters for display and for student reference.

How to start a letter

Less formal	More formal	
Dear Maria	Dear Mrs Dileo	**contractions:**
Dear Mr Jones	Dear Editor	**Mr, Mrs, Ms**
Dear Aunty Flora	Dear Ms F Garden	**initial capital**
Dear Uncle Jim	Dear Sir or Madam	**letter for each**
Dear Granny	Dear Sir/Madam	**word**

Closing a letter

The closure is in keeping with the start of the letter. Model and discuss ways to close letters before students choose their own way of closing the letter. Ways of closing can be added to the letter writing display.

How to close a letter

Less formal	More formal	
Regards	Yours sincerely	**capital letter**
Best wishes	Yours faithfully	**for the first**
See you soon		**word only, all**
Sincerely		**other words**
		are lower case

Using people's titles in letters and on envelopes

The students bring examples of letters and envelopes to form a display. Group together similar letters and envelopes, drawing students' attention to the features of each type; e.g. formal, informal, invitations, advertising and so on. (Always read all letters before displaying to avoid insensitive comments being made public.)

Titles

Men without any other title are addressed as Mr, women without any other title can be addressed in one of three ways — Miss, Mrs or Ms — depending on personal preference. When in doubt, use Ms.

Other ways of addressing people include:

- Dr (Doctor), Fr (Father), Sr (Sister), Br (Brother): these shortened forms are contractions and as they end with the last letter of the word and do not have full stops.
- Lady, Sir, Bishop, Archbishop and Rabbi.

Use open punctuation on envelopes: capital letters only, no commas or full stops. (Australia Post prefers all letters to be addressed using open punctuation as it speeds up the sorting process.) Leave a space for the stamp and the postmark. If you write too close to the top of the envelope the postmark may be printed over the address.

Model addressing envelopes on both sides and then the students can practise addressing some of their own.

Front of the envelope

Mr F Brown
Proprietor
Happy Pets Shop
Villewood NSW 0987

Write your name as the sender on the back of the envelope

Sender: Ms A Wolf
6 Railway Place
Villewood NSW 0987

Capital letters used for the initial letter in people's names, in place names, and for states and territories.

DIALOGUE and SCRIPTWRITING

Dialogue is written to imitate or record real speech. A simple of understanding dialogue is to say that it is 'talk' written down. To help make speech sound natural, writers often use contractions, slang or colloquialisms. Dialogue records the words used between two or more people. For natural dialogue the writer needs to use language that is appropriate for the speaker. For example, an elderly person would not use today's classroom slang. If a story is formal, it will have language which is polite and correct. Informal language is often chatty and less precise. While the choice of words is great, words chosen must be appropriate to the character and setting.

There are many sources of dialogue and these can range from fiction to non-fiction. Dialogue can be based on real or imagined experiences, or can be found in picture story books, humorous stories, poems, fantasy, folk and fairytales, historical characters, novels, science fiction, videos, films, cartoon strips, radio and television. Draw attention to the differences between the grammar of spoken English and the grammar of written English.

How to write realistic dialogue

To help students write realistic dialogue, they need time to reflect on the six 'what they' statements.

> what they did
> what they saw
> what they felt
> what they thought
> what they said
> what they heard

Write the six 'what they' statements on a sheet of paper with a large space underneath for the students to fill in. Select a setting for which dialogue is required. This could include stories, poems and journal entries written by students as starting points. Consider this exchange between a person buying shoes and a sales assistant.

> *Sales assistant:* Good afternoon. May I help you?
>
> *Customer:* Good afternoon, you may. I'm looking for a pair of black slip on shoes to wear to a party.
>
> *Sales assistant:* Certainly. What size do you take?
>
> *Customer:* I'm not sure. Maybe it's size 10.
>
> *Sales assistant:* I'll measure your feet to make sure. Would you please take off your shoes?

Students can perform role plays to help them write realistic dialogue. Other students can record what happened under the six 'what they' statements.

Give students practice in writing scenes before moving on to acts, and if really adventurous, a one-act play. Remember to set a time limit for the performance.

Editing the dialogue script

Editing scripts is a very important part of dialogue writing. Choose one of the students' scripts. The writer of the script can give a brief synopsis of the plot to set the scene then provide copies of the script for each member of the pair/group. After the script has been read silently and then performed, students can suggest how the script could be improved. Students mark (in pencil) the changes they think are desirable and why. (For example, the change would sound better; it uses fewer words; the character would not have used that word anyway; it clarifies the story or what is happening.) The students and teacher can present their ideas to the writer. The writer as 'owner' of this script is not bound to accept the ideas. The writer may explain why the script was written that way.

Pose questions such as these for the group to consider:
- How does it sound?
- Does it sound like real people talking?
- Do the words flow or are they stilted?
- Does it need to be edited?

Discuss what could be changed and, with the writer's permission, change the draft script. Read the revised dialogue. If the writer agrees, the changes can be written in as the new dialogue.

Students may have problems developing a script because the characters they have written about do not seem compelling or real. Students can build the strength of their characters by:
- wider reading about characters to help develop detail
- using characters based on those in books
- writing character profiles that include personal details (name, address, occupation); physical description; likes and dislikes; character's age; how they get on with other people; would you like to meet them; general interests.

Speakers have to say something that is interesting. If characters are from another place or time, background reading at the local/school library or other research such as watching movies is needed. When discussing books in class, give students practice in building character profiles. The easiest profiles to build up are from folk tales that have sufficiently interesting dialogue; e.g. *Cinderella* or *Hansel and Gretel*.

Punctuation in dialogue (")

Double quotation marks are used to show the exact words used by a speaker. The used may not form a complete sentence.

> "I'm extremely happy that you have come," the old man said.
>
> When I last saw him he said, "Come back next year."
>
> "Where is he?" he asked the policeman. "He's not here!" she said in amazement.

Single quotation marks can be used to show the name of a newspaper or journal that has been used as the background for a news article or item; e.g. 'The Sydney Morning Herald' but only in handwriting. In printed texts, titles are written in italics.

Note that quotation marks are sometimes called speech marks by the children.

Question marks (?)

A question mark signals that a question has been asked.

Direct questions
> *How many boys went?*
> *You really went there?*
> *Where are the pencils? the maps? the torches?*

Indirect questions do not have question marks
> *She was asked whether she really wanted it.*

Some demands require a question mark
> *Will you kindly give it to me?*

Questions of doubt:
North Sydney won the competition last year?

Exclamation marks (!)

An exclamation mark signals a high degree of surprise, indignation or incredulity. It can show strong emotion. It is not the mark that conveys the emotion but the exclamation itself.

She won the car raffle!
I can't believe you!
You wouldn't dare!

It can be used as an **interjection**
God bless you!
Good health!

Writing a script? Read this first

Scripts:
- need to be self-contained and do not require the audience to provide additional information to make sense of the story
- start with picture story-books
- establish the elements of structure, climax and setting
- use stories, poems and journal entries written by students as starting points for script development
- can give a brief synopsis of what has happened so far and where the storyline starts
- give the reader instructions about the voice to be used, action and other directions (use round brackets to indicate these)
- maintain a balance between the exchanges of two or more characters; one character doing all the talking is a monologue and is usually a narrative or a reflection.
- should only use monologues sparingly
- can use poetry as dialogue as it is usually has some form of metre.

How to publish a script?

Use a computer to 'publish' a script. Use a range of font types, print sizes and ways of formatting: plain, bold, italic, underlining, outline and shadow. These enable scripts to be produced in a very polished and professional way. Avoid using too many different fonts in one piece.

Design folders in which to place scripts. Leave a wide margin on the side (the gutter) so the binding does not cover the script.

ACTIVITIES

Creating a character profile

Create a character you are familiar with, or about whom you have enough information to write their dialogue. Actual photographs can be useful prompts in writing about a character. Personalities in popular magazines or in books are a good source of material. To build a profile, make a set of personal documents for a character: name, address, date of birth, occupation, marital status, driver's license, credit cards, passports, likes and dislikes, favourite quotes, what the character is reading at the moment.

Character Profile: The White Witch — The Queen of Narnia

Name	The White Witch — The Queen of Narnia
Address	The Castle, Narnia, The Ice Kingdom
Date of birth	Not known. Thought to be many millennia ago
Occupation	Queen and ruler
Marital status	Not known.
Driver's licence	Does not drive. Has a fat, three feet high dwarf as a driver.
Credit cards	None. Pays cash.

Passport	Royal and diplomatic
Likes	Snow and ice, white fur, and golden wands
Dislikes	Sons of Adam and daughters of Eve
Favourite quote	'Are you a great overgrown dwarf that has cut off its beard?'
Reading	How to Freeze the World.

Source: *The Lion, the Witch and the Wardrobe*, C.S. Lewis

My character's journal

Keep a journal of a character to show a day, a week, or a month in his or her life. Choose characters who take part in interesting, exciting and believeable activites.

> A day in the Journal of Hannah Tupper, a character found in the book, *The Witch of the Blackbird Pond* (Elizabeth George Speare).
>
> Tuesday: In my meadow I met a girl who was crying. When she saw me I knew she thought that I was a witch. I saw her body stiffen. I offered her some food and she came back to my house. I told her I had a seafaring friend who visits me when he comes back from voyages.

Cartoon dialogue

Model writing dialogue. Collect cartoon strips that have more than four frames and have feature characters. White out the dialogue in the speech balloons or cover it with adhesive strips then photocopy and distribute to students. (You may need to enlarge the cartoon.) Students write a story that fits the number of frames and is appropriate for the pictures. Who are the characters? What are they doing? What are they saying? Is this serious or humorous?

Students can write the story first with sentences for each frame. Then the sentences can be used to write the dialogue in the speech balloons.

Stories with dialogue

Students write a simple story of five, eight or ten lines using a theme or describing an event (see the example below). The story must have at least two characters. Students draw the characters in frames and add speech bubbles for the dialogue, which tells the story.

> Simon and Peter went on a journey seeking the end of the rainbow. They met a wizard who offered them money if they helped him get his treasure from a nasty dragon.
> They followed him into the mountains and had to go over many treacherous paths.
> There were great dangers on the way.
> A giant serpent tried to eat them.
> A huge spider dropped its web on them.
> At last they came to the cave, which was guarded by the fire-breathing dragon.
> They tricked the dragon and got the treasure.

Writing new dialogue

Students bring their favourite cartoon strip to class. (Keep a copy of the original to compare the changes.) Write out their dialogue or cover it over, then photocopy the strip and swap with other students who write a dialogue. When completed, distribute the original cartoon strip for comparison. Display the original and the new version and leave space for students to write their comments.

Students are familiar with many stories; e.g. *Goldilocks and the Three Bears*, and the dialogue that occurs between the characters. Now revise the dialogue with the students. Variations can be made to the story; by introducing a new character, changing the setting of the story, or changing the beginning, the middle or the end of the story. Find different versions of the story and encourage students to look at them. In groups, students can read and retell the different versions, noting the different texts used. Each group can decide which aspect of the story it will change. The rewriting of the story and altered dialogue can be done on white paper, the whiteboard, typed into a Word document, or recorded by a student. The dialogue needs to be read very carefully to maintain consistency of plot, setting, action and character. (Try to vary the ways students write and share their work.) It is important that the students revise the story, that they are quite clear where changes will be made, and how changes may affect other details in the story. For example, if the setting of *Goldilocks and the Three Bears* is changed to an Asian country, the bears may be eating rice porridge or tofu.

While students are reworking details and aspects of stories, focus on linguistic features such as:

- Punctuation: capitals are used in titles, names of people and places, and for and the first word of each new speaker. Titles of plays, films, videos and television use capitals and are underlined if handwritten, but in italics if typed; e.g. *The Importance of Being Ernest*.
- Colons (:) are used outside the dialogue.
- Ellipsis is used (…) to show faltering speech or to suggest reluctance. Note only three points are used.
- Sentence structure: a variety of clauses will be used, but these may often represent spoken language rather than the clauses and sentences of standard written English.
- Coordinating conjunctions *and, but, or, yet* are used.
- Subordinating conjunctions are used.
- Direct speech is a recording of what exactly was said.
- A new line is started when a different character starts to talk.
- Contractions may be used.
- Colloquialisms may be used.

DIARY and JOURNAL WRITING

Recording experiences

Diary and journal entries, a writer's notebook, daybooks, learning logs and subject journals are part of the writing process and are a valuable record of the students' developing responses to their experiences. Diary and journal entries are part of the students' expanding writing folio and part of the writing conference.

Writer's notebook
It is a record of personal experiences — a small notebook of impressions, feelings and thoughts. Jottings can be used later as a source for writing. Professional writers usually carry a notebook for jotting down things which they later use in their writing.

Diary and journal writing
Diary writing is part of pre-writing and gives students an opportunity to experiment with many types of texts, such as different forms of poetry; e.g. humorous, shaped and rhyming poems.

Diary entries need not always be written as a narrative; complete sentences are not necessary; e.g. "Huge red balloons in the sky." They can be written as a line of poetry; e.g. "a golden host of daffodils."

Encourage students to be inventive in their recording. Perhaps recording information as limericks or using a group of rhyming words; e.g. "I held on to the *kite* with all my might but it flew *right* out of *sight*."

They can practise onomatopoeia (sound words) to describe events; e.g. Wet washing on the clothesline:

> *Slicking, slicking then slunkety.*
> *Slopping, slopping, wetly round.*
> *Slishing, slishing, slowly, slowly*
> *Flopperty, flopperty on to the ground.*

Students can record interesting conversations they have overheard; e.g. "Really, what people say. You'd think that they would have more sense." Alternatively, they could record the words of a song, or a title of a book or a poem they find appealing.

In a diary or journal there should be examples of sustained writing that vary from single sentences with young students to more than a full page for older students.

A subject journal, a learning log or a day book

This is a learning diary in which students keep a personal account of learning in particular subjects. These accounts or reflections can be kept as part of the student's work in that subject or they can be kept in addition to a journal or a diary.

A subject journal could be each student's record, e.g. of the growth of seeds in the classroom. The student would be required to measure the seedlings as they grow and to record information correctly, recording factually and accurately what is happening.

Subject Journal

Day	Entry	Annotation
Day 1	We planted our seeds at 2.00 p.m. exactly 2 cm deep. I watered them.	past tense
Day 5	The seeds haven't shown any growth. I reckon they've rotted.	contractions
Day 7	A very small green tip on the top of the soil.	
Day 12	The tip is now a leaf and now there are two tips.	coordinating conjunction / two independent clauses
Day 15	I think there is a bud.	
Day 20	There are now two buds. The leafs measure 7 cm each.	spelling approximation

Discuss with students why they will be keeping a diary or a journal. Encourage students to have diaries or journals on hand to record ideas, to use their diaries and journals as resources, and also to see that writing for themselves provides an opportunity to develop ideas, thoughts and issues with greater clarity and precision. Model the many ways a diary or journal can kept. You may need to start keeping a diary that records impressions and ideas to be shared with the class. Through this diary you can model many ideas for students to use.

Keeping a diary or a journal is closely related to personal letter writing because it is where the writer often records very personal information, important feelings and reactions. Teachers must respect these aspects in a student's diary.

Help students keep their diaries organised by showing them:
- ways of recording information
- how to start each new entry on a new page and how to date each entry, which will enable the student to come back at another time to write further
- how a ring notebook enables further pages to be added if a student wishes to write at length.

Students can write about:
- what the weather is like
- the kind of day they're having
- something special which is going to happen soon
- which teams won at the weekend
- what they like to do
- what they're going to do at the weekend

Diary

Monday 16	Practice for school play after school	punctuation left out
Tuesday 17	Late for school bus. Mum drove me and she wasn't too happy about it. **Although she did.**	sentence fragment
Wednesday 18	School excursion to Smith's farm. The bus trip was OK but the farm really **ponged**. John **chundered** and we all laughed.	
Thursday 19	The **principle** threw a real turn over our class's manners yesterday when John had a **chuck** in the bus on the way back.	spelling approximati colloquilalisms
Friday 20	Went to Youth Club as it was August sports night.	
Saturday 21	Dad took Clare and me to the footy and my team won.	

A diary entry

> 2 November 2022
>
> Dear Diary
> Today I had a really good time. The new girl in my class asked me to her house to play. Mum said that I could go but to be on my best **behaviur**. There house is fabulous. It's pretty new so everything looked good. She has her own phone.

- open style punctuation
- spelling approximation
- usage confusion

Remember:
- Provide students with time each week to write their journals.
- Journals can be written during the students' writing time or at other times.
- When beginning to keep journals, work with small groups of students each week until they are comfortable and confident writing journals.
- Work with all students, not just with those whom you think need help.
- Some students may need to continue working with the teacher for some time.
- Diaries and journals can make it easier for reticent students to show their learning and development.
- Student development, which can often go unnoticed, can be seen in a diary as it is a record over time.
- Parts of diaries and journals can form part of the student's ongoing assessment.

Provide copies of published diaries and journals of famous and not so famous men and women in the classroom for students to read. These can be models for their writing. (Include fictitious diaries.)

Penny Pollard's Letters, Robin Klein
So Much To Tell You, John Marsden
The Diary of Anna Frank, Anna Frank
Eleanor, Elizabeth, Libby Gleeson
The Secret Diary of Adrian Mole, Sue Townsend

Text types for subject journals or learning logs

Here are examples of different types of recording

Report writing

> Two final contestants in the annual poetry writing competition this year are brother and sister John and Julie Craddock. They are both very excited to be finalists and wished each other well. The competition will be held at St James Church Hall on Tuesday 18 August at 7.00 p.m.

Writing summaries

To make ice cubes you need a tray which can be placed in a freezer Fill tray with water and place in a freezer. Do not overfill trays. Allow sufficient time to freeze.

> **Interview**
>
> *Reporter:* Mrs James, you have just returned from climbing the Andes. Why did you climb the Andes?
> *Mrs James:* Well, for many years I had lead a very ordinary life as a wife and mother, and then one day I decided to do what I had always wanted to do and that was climb some very high faraway mountains and so off I went.

Research reports

Canis Minor, which is Latin for 'lesser dog', is a small constellation found in the sky near the equator. *Canis Minor*, which is near Orion, is known as one of Orion's hunting dogs.

Surveys

Students surveyed in Grade 6 at Rainbow Primary School were asked the question: 'Should homework be compulsory in years 5 and 6?' The survey results:

Agreed 50%
Disagreed 40%
Undecided 10%

When told of the results the principal said, "Homework is important because it teaches students to learn to study systematically and regularly." The survey will be conducted again in six months time.

Mini profile

A mini profile can be made of a teacher at the school, the school secretary, principal, a parent helper, a local shopkeeper, the crossing person and others.

Mini Profile of Sue Jonas

School secretary Sue Jonas has been working at the school since 2015. She has worked in offices and schools. She will be on leave during Term 3.

Childhood ambitions?
To be a juggler.

How did you become a secretary?
I found that if I wanted to make a living I had to find something else to do.

Do you have a family?
Yes, I have three children, two boys and a girl.

Do you like working at the school?
Yes, I'm very happy here; the students and staff are very friendly.

A mini profile can also be developed where the reader has to guess the person's identity.

Write a self-portrait

Discuss with students descriptions of characters they have come across in their reading. Find some descriptions of characters in novels and other print material then discuss what the characters are like. Encourage students to use adjectives, adjectival phrases and adjectival clauses. They can make a list of words and phrases to describe the characters and list their feelings about the characters at the beginning and at the end of the book. (Have they changed?) This should enable students to build a profile of their favourite character.

Students can then list adjectives to describe themselves. They can list action verbs to tell what kinds of things they do; e.g. play football (run, mark, kick, tackle) or play tennis. They can use the list of words to write a self-portrait. Other students can draw a portrait of the writer from the written description.

This is what I heard

Double quotation marks (" ") are used to enclose the actual words said by a speaker; e.g.

Dr Livingston said: "Yes, I've returned from exploring upper Africa and might I say a more beautiful country I have never seen before."

Students can record real conversations in their diaries. A colon used with quotation marks indicates that a quote or reported speech is to follow. They can record snippets of conversations that are heard in the street, or in the playground; e.g.

Mark: "We went to Circus Oz last night. It was fantastic."

Real conversation provides a rich source of authentic dialogue that can be used in narratives and scriptwriting.

full stops are used inside the quotation marks.

No quotation marks are needed when dialogue is in script.

What can I smell? see? hear?

Encourage students to become sensitive to sounds, smells, sights and textures in their environment by recording impressions and feelings aroused. Students can use a variety of headings to encourage their ideas.

New sounds
slurping a melting icypole
ice cubes on tiles
a clash of thunder late at night
grandpa snoring

Startling smells
my sister's cooking
dad's new brew
a rubbish bin on a hot day
my lunch box unopened for days

Stunning sights
Collingwood winning the grand final
brilliant fireworks over water

Smooth textures
old jeans
my young kitten's fur

Adjectives to describe sounds
clinking chains
creaking doors
ten wet sheets slapping in the wind

Autumn smells
earthy, dank leaves
smoke in the air
freshly-made soup

Model paragraphs using verbs: in the present tense, the past tense, the continuous tense, future tense and the past perfect tense. Also model with adverbs to describe how an action is performed; e.g. quickly, slowly, languidly.

Present tense

Let us walk along the path that goes to the river as I want to see the rowers in their boats.

Past tense

Yesterday I went with my friend along the path that goes to the river as I wanted to see the rowers in their boats.

Continuous tense

I was walking with my friend along the path that goes to the river as I was wanting to see the rowers in their boats.

Future tense

Tomorrow I will walk along the path that goes to the river as I want to see the rowers in their boats.

Past perfect tense

I had walked along the path that goes to the river as I wanted to see the rowers in their boats.

Build up lists for spring, summer, autumn and winter smells, sounds, sights and textures. Fill in the lists over time. Students then write sentences or paragraphs describing what they can smell, feel, see or touch, for example:

> *On an autumn morning the air can be dry with the dust of crushed leaves.*
>
> *In summer I can see a heat haze over the hills.*

Improvising on a text

Students write their own poems or songs based on favourite poems and songs:

The Man From Snowy River, A. B. Paterson

> *There was movement at the station, for the word had passed around*
> *That the colt from the old Regret had got away,*

becomes:

> There was movement on the tarmac,
> for information had passed around
> That the night plane from Sydney ← capital letters
> had got away,
> And was up in the bright blue sky –
> it was worth twenty million dollars, ← adjectives
> So all the stickybeaks had gathered
> from far and near
> The gossips ready to see and tell had
> clustered at the airport ← verbs
> For the idle love a good time when it's
> free and open to all
> And the kiosk owner smiles with
> delight as she takes the money from
> all sorts.

Students keep a progress report of what they have learnt, what they want to find out about or what they need to learn. Students can head up pages; e.g. "What I have learnt in computers so far." All areas of the curriculum are useful as starters. This example has verbs in bold.

What I have learnt in computers so far

I **learned** about bits and bytes, and I **write** using the keyboard. My writing **is stored** on the hard drive.

Diary of a character from a book

Students can keep a journal or diary of a character in a book they are reading; e.g.

Space Demons, Gillian Rubinstein
Halfway Across the Galaxy and Turn Left, Robin Klein
The Eighteenth Emergency, Betsy Byars

Diary of Andrew from <u>Space Demons</u>

When I saw Mario Ferrone I thought why do I need to keep out of his way he's not that tough. Like everyone else at Kingsgate I had kept people out of his way. I gave John his brother back his bike I had 'borrowed'. John said it was OK. Mario said that I had stolen it. Mario started to fight me. We were on the ground and Mario had me as he kicked and fought all-out with no holds barred.

---

capitals used to begin proper nouns, place names, names of people

pronouns: *I* first person or third person *he/she*

book titles underlined

Diary and journal writing

Diary of a person who lived in an imaginary land

Develop diaries of people who have lived in imaginary lands. Research will need to be done to ensure credibility. Linguistic features will include verbs in the past tense.

Provide students with a list of books which they may choose to read:

> *Harry Potter and the Philosopher's Stone,* JK Rowling
> *The Halfman of O,* Maurice Gee
> *The Dark is Rising,* Susan Cooper
> *Dragonsong,* Anne McCaffrey
> *Chronicles of Prydain,* Lloyd Alexander

Horoscope

Students can collect horoscopes from magazines and newspapers. They use these to compile a list of star signs and what are said to be the attributes of people born under the various star signs. (Stress that horoscopes cannot be taken seriously.) Model these with students. Students can write their own horoscope, but they are not to put their names to it. Display the horoscope and ask students to identify who they think wrote it and why.

My horoscope

Scorpio, 24 Oct–22 Nov

Don't expect everything to go well for you. Remember Rome wasn't built in a day. But during the next few weeks you will find obstacles in your way. Don't despair, your good luck is not running out. You need to rise to the challenges and muster up your patience and strength.

For your information: sign posts

These are not punctuation marks but symbols commonly used in written work.

An **asterisk (*)** is used to highlight sentences or items.

* Close to public transport.

An **ampersand (&)** is used in some instances to join two items together, such as the name of a business firm; e.g. Waller & Chin. It is read as '*and*.' It can be used in the names of joint authors when using the Harvard system of referencing. It cannot be used as an alternative for '*and*' in written text unless the ampersand is part of a registered trade name; e.g. K P & M.

A **solidus (/)** is also known as a slash or a diagonal and is used:

- to indicate alternatives: *boy/girl; and/or*
- for some abbreviations: *a/c* (account); *c/-* (care of)
- to show a fraction in mathematical expressions: *1/10; km/hr*

The **hatch (#)** has come into use in recent times; most touch telephones have a hatch key and it is found on modern Qwerty keyboards. It is used to indicate numbers:

- in addresses #147 Smith St Newtown
- in telephone numbers #213 4567

Italics are used for writing book titles (use underlining in handwriting). For example, in italics Paul Jenning's *Uncanny*, underlined Paul Jenning's Uncanny.

An **ellipsis** (...) has three points and is used:

- to indicate reluctance, or irony, or faltering speech; e.g. "Oh ... Oh ... but that's not right."
- to show missing words in quoted matter: "All teachers ... must ensure that all students ... before and after school."

Note:

Only three points of ellipsis are used even when the ellipsis comes at the end of a sentence.

PART B
TEACHING THE LANGUAGE OF GRAMMAR

A brief introduction to grammar and vocabulary

There are as many definitions of grammar as there are theories of linguistics. As well, there is a view that grammar is all about using some long-held rules or expectations about how language works. You can find more about this dimension of usage and expectation in Fowler (1965), Strunk & White (1979; 2000) and Campbell & Ryles (2018).

Of greater use in teaching students about the grammar of writing is a focus upon the **patterns of language**, the *phrases, clauses and groups* that are used by speakers in their utterances (what they say) and in their sentences (what they write). Phrases, clauses and groups are the patterns in which words function to create the structure and meaning of communication and are thus the first layer of instruction and information about grammar for writing and reading.

The **parts of speech** are the second layer of grammar instruction and learning. There are two sets of parts of speech.

The first set are the **open-class** or **vocabulary parts of speech: nouns, verbs, adjectives** and **adverbs**. These are the words that carry meaning and are grouped as noun-verb (*dogs eat*), adjective-noun (*hungry dogs*), verb adverb (*eat greedily*). There are more than 500,000 of these vocabulary words, but most people only need 20,000 to 30,000 words and their derivatives. (For example, *derivation* is a *derivative* of *derive*.) Words come from Old English (Anglo-Saxon), Norse languages, Norman French, Latin, Greek and from every language of refugees and migrants who went to live in Britain as well as countries that were part of the trading and empire of Britain from the early 17th century to the middle of the 20th century. Teaching vocabulary is a vital part of the teaching of grammar.

The second set of parts of speech are the **closed-class** or **grammar** or **functional parts of speech**. There are about 120 of these words across four parts of speech: **prepositions, conjunctions, pronouns** and **determiners**. Then we add another 20 or so verbs (*being* and *having verbs*) and modal verbs such as *could* and *should*. Almost all of these words are from the Old English of the Germanic invaders and settlers who came to Britannia after the Romans retreated. These peoples gave England its name and its language, and the grammatical parts of speech, the words that make the language function, are mostly from their language of more than 1500 years ago.

The grammatical and vocabulary parts of speech (i.e. all eight parts of speech) function together in the patterns of phrases, clauses and groups. When we write down those words and patterns, we have to use punctuation to mark the boundaries of meaning that are carried by intonation in spoken language. The essential element of written language is that well-marked larger pattern called the **sentence**. The best definition of a sentence is that it has a capital letter and a full stop.

SENTENCES

The English **sentence** is marked in writing by boundary markers such as the **capital letter** at the beginning and a **full stop** (or ? or !) at the end. **Clauses** and **phrases**, however, are features of both spoken and written English. A sentence may contain one or more clauses, and can be classified according to the relationship between the clauses.

Sentences can be statements or declarations, questions, exclamations or commands. Speakers will often use sentences of one word (*Really!* and one phrase (*At dawn?*), and these will be reflected in written language in dialogue. In written English, one word and one-phrase sentences are used sparingly, and only for effect and style.

The clause is the basic structure for expressing meaning, and consists of a **subject** and **predicate** (Also known as topic and comment.)

The car	*is in the garage*
subject	predicate
topic	comment

Other examples of simple sentences (one-clause sentences) are:

The smaller children *are watching television.*
The old man *walks to the shop at midday.*

The subject or topic is in bold type in each sentence or clause. The rest of the sentence provides the predicate, the comment on the topic. A further feature has been added to the topic by using the qualifying words *smaller* and *old*. There are also qualifying statements in the comment that provide further information: *in the garage, at midday,* and *to the shop.*

Further information can be added to the topic and comment through the use of phrases. Clauses can be combined with each other so that a number of topics and their comments can be combined in the one sentence.

Punctuation: full stop

A full stop is used to signal the end of a sentence.

command: *Go to the cupboard and get my coat.*
statement: *We have agreed to buy the house.*
indirect question: *My only question is where did she get it.*

Examples of the **correct use** of a full stop are:
- days
  Sunday, Monday, Tuesday, Wednesday, Thursday, Friday, Saturday are abbreviated to: *Sun. Mon. Tues. Wed. Thurs. Fri. Sat.* and written with a full stop
- months
  January, February, March, April, May, June, July, August, September, October, November, December are abbreviated to: *Jan. Feb. Mar. Apr. Aug. Sept. Oct. Nov. Dec.* and written with a full stop. But May, June and July should not be abbreviated.
- dates: Use a full stop when written entirely in figures: 13.09.22 or 13.09.2022

The full stop is not used in the following instances:
- at the end of the title of a book or a poem
- after dates or signatures
- after contractions: vols Fr Dept St Rd (end with last letter of the word)
- after symbols of measurement or currency: km g Hz
- after acronyms: ANZAC UNESCO
- after an abbreviation: GPO USA UK Drive—Dr Crescent—Cres Place—Pl (used in addresses)
- after contractions of Australian states and territories, except * below
Northern Territory NT
New South Wales NSW
Australian Capital Territory ACT
Victoria Vic.*
South Australia SA
Western Australia WA
Tasmania Tas.*
Queensland Qld
and Commonwealth Cwlth
Note that Qld and Cwlth are contractions. The others are abbreviations. Note that Vic. and Tas. each have a full stop.
- after the abbreviations of foreign countries
United Kingdom UK
New Zealand NZ
United States of America USA
- after ordinal numbers
1st 2nd 3rd 4th 5th 19th
21 August 2020 24 October 2022
Note: *th* is no longer the preferred use in dates.

ACTIVITIES

One

The objective of this sentence activity is to allow students to use their knowledge of word order and clausal structures in spoken English to develop sentences.

Start the pattern with one word. The students add words in turn until a sentence is completed. Write the completed sentences on the board or on butcher's paper for later reading, discussion and dissection.

For example:

i) My ...
    My puppy ...
    My puppy likes ...

ii) My birthday is ...

iii) My name is ..... and I like playing ... and eating ....

Two

List five words and ask the students to use all five words in a sentence in the sequence given. (They will need to add words to those given.)

children mice when nibble cheese
Children are like mice when they nibble cheese.

You can increase the number of words, but ask students to write a story. You can then check for poor use of boundary markers, run-on sentences and other difficulties in sentence formation.

PHRASES

A **phrase** is any group or pattern of words. Some examples of phrases are:

***in** the street*	prepositional phrases
***on** the ball*	(see Prepositions)
***after** dark*	
***up** the creek*	
*a **car***	noun phrase/group
a green car	adjectival phrase/noun group
***Australian** swimmers*	adjectival phrase/noun group
***very** fast*	adverbial phrase
*very **fast** car*	adjectival phrase/noun group
was going to see	verb phrase

This is only one way of classifying phrases. The particular name of the phrase comes from one of the contributing parts of speech in the phrase. The part of speech that gives the phrase its name is in bold type.

Another term used instead of phrase is **group** (Halliday, 1985).

Note:
A noun group is any group of works that contains a noun. In the prepositional phrases above, the noun group is inside the prepositional phrase; e.g. *in the street* (prepositional phrase), *the street* (noun group).

In the adjectival phrases, the noun is the more important word, so it is preferrable to teach the adjectival phrase (in these examples) as noun groups.

CLAUSES

Clauses are groups of words that contain a **verb**. Often a clause is introduced by a **conjunction**. There are two major types of clauses: **independent** and **dependent**. A special type of dependent clause is the adjectival clause (called relative clause in the US). There are also **incomplete** clauses and **complete** clauses. An incomplete clause has an incomplete verb.

Independent clauses and coordinating conjunctions

An **independent clause** is one that can stand independently. The test for independence is to ask if the clause statement can make sense without the need for further information. The following clauses are independent:

> Mary and John went to the city.
> They caught the train.
> They were able to go to the movies.

Independent clauses can be joined together by using **coordinating**

conjunctions: *and, but, or, nor, so, for, yet.* (See Conjunctions.)
Mary and John caught the early train and they went to the city. They went to the movies but Mary did not like the show.

Note:
An independent clause is also a complete clause because the verb in the clause is a complete (finite) verb.

Read the sentences below. Note the use of the **coordinating conjunctions** *and, but* and *or*.

The car is in the garage **and** *the petrol tank is empty.*
The car is in the garage **but** *the tyre is flat.*
The car is in the garage **or** *John is driving it.*

You will notice that:
- The coordinating conjunctions join the two clauses.
- On each side there is a subject and predicate (topic and comment).
- Each clause can be written independently of the other.
- The coordinating conjunction is used to join two sentences or clauses that can stand independently of each other.
- The conjunctions create new meanings in the relationship of one clause to the other. (See Coordinating conjunctions.)

For your information:
These types of sentences are called compound sentences.

Dependent clauses and subordinating conjunctions

Dependent clauses cannot stand on their own. They need to be with an independent clause to gain meaning. **Complete** dependent clauses begin with a **subordinating conjunction**. (Many of these clauses are also known as **adverbial clauses** since these clauses function grammatically as adverbs.)

Sentences containing dependent clauses are called complex sentences.

*He had an accident **because** he had driven too fast.*
*The children went to the party **where** they had a good time.*
*They stayed at the beach **until** the sun went down.*

ACTIVITIES

One

Have a number of small cards (10 cm x 5 cm) with a different subordinating conjunction written on each. Give one to each student, together with a strip of paper 50 cm x 5 cm. Each student will then have a conjunction and a strip of paper.

| when |
| where |
| if |
| until |
| since |
| however |
| unless |
| as |
| before |

Ask students to complete the following sentence:

They went to the cinema _____.

Place the beginning of the sentence on the board. Then place one of the students' clauses after it. Place a selection of other clauses under the first dependent clause.

They went to the cinema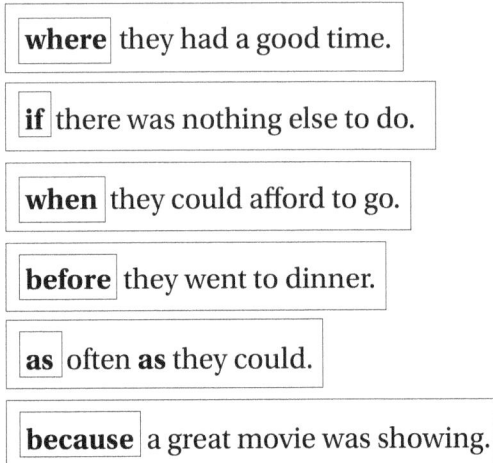

Discuss the various sentences that have been produced. Note that some conjunctions could not be used after the opening independent or main clause. For example, *if*, *whether* and *unless* function better when put first, before the independent clause.

For your information:
Sentences that begin with an independent clause are called loose sentences.

Place the dependent clauses in front of the independent clause. Ask the students to tell you what can be used after the dependent clause when it appears first in the sentence. (Answer: A comma.) Demonstrate the rule with the remaining clauses.

| **If** | there was nothing to do | , they went to the cinema.

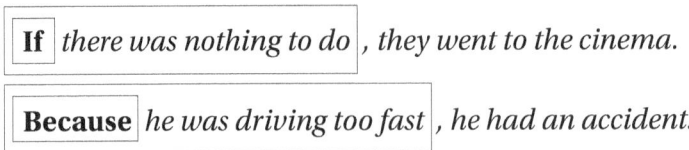

Two

Ask the students to complete the following sentences on strips of paper.

> *He had an accident **because** _____.*
> *They went to the festival **where** _____.*
> *She kept looking **until** _____.*

Ask the students to read out their clauses beginning with the words in bold type. Can each of these clauses stand alone or independently from the first clause?

Ask the students to cut the sentence after the independent clause, then reverse the position of the clauses. Again, note the use of the comma.

You will notice that:
- The clauses beginning with the subordinating conjunctions (in bold type) are dependent upon the other clauses they are paired with.
- Subordinating conjunctions introduce and join dependent clauses.
- When the dependent clause comes first, it is separated from the independent clause by a comma.
- Sentences beginning with dependent clauses are known as periodic sentences.

Dependent clauses (incomplete)

You will get three kinds of response from this activity. Each response provides you with data for use in three areas of language study:
1. The relationship between an incomplete and complete dependent clause
2. The **dangling modifier** or **hanging participle**
3. The **noun group**.

The relationship between an incomplete and complete dependent clause

There is a special group of dependent clauses that do not have conjunctions and complete verbs.

driving too fast   present participle form
having eaten a big breakfast   past participle form
to see the sunset   infinitive form

Note:
The verbs in these clauses are incomplete, and are based upon the **participle** (participial) form (present and past) and the **infinitive** form of the verb.

Give the clauses to the students on a worksheet, and ask them to complete each sentence. Many students will produce independent clauses:

Driving too fast, the man had an accident.
Having eaten a big breakfast, the children went out to play.
To see the sunset, you must look towards the west.

You will find that a number of students will place a comma after the incomplete clause, showing that they understand the previous rule about the use of the comma when the dependent clause starts the sentence.

Alternatively, present the incomplete clauses on strips of paper and get students to complete the sentences on the strips. Each strip will need to be 70 cm x 5 cm.

Take a pair of scissors and cut the incomplete dependent clause from the front and place it after the main or independent clause. Ask the students to complete the sentence so that it makes sense.

> *The man had an accident because he was driving too fast.*
> *The children went out to play when they had eaten a big breakfast.*
> *You must look towards the west if you want to see the sunset.*

Discuss the results, pointing out to the students that often you must change the incomplete clause into a complete clause for the sentence to sound like English, or to give it greater emphasis. The last example shows the greater emphasis in using the conjunction *if* and making the verb complete.

Mention that as a general principle, the complete clause has a complete (or finite) verb, and a conjunction.

Three
The dangling modifier or hanging participle

Note:
These forms of incomplete clause present problems for students.

Complete the following sentences:

> *Turning the car in the street, _____.*
> *Hearing the bell for the end of the lunch break, _____.*

Some students will produce sentences that do not make sense, and which are comical. Reverse the order of the independent and dependent clauses, and the students will see how they can fix the problem.

> *Turning the car in the street, the dog ran away.*
>
> *The dog ran away as (we) <u>turned</u> the car in the street.*

Each of these clauses has a subject (to be determined) and is dependent on another clause which has yet to be written.

Hearing the bell for the end of the lunch break, the children stopped playing.

The verbs *turning* and *hearing* are incomplete, and may need to be used with *is* or one of its derivatives (*are, was, were, am, be*) in order to be a complete verb.

The children stopped playing when they <u>heard</u> the bell for the end of the lunch break.

Note: The past tense of the verbs.

Four
The noun group

From the first activity on incomplete clauses, some students have produced the following sentences.

Driving too fast is dangerous.
To see the sunset is a great thing to do.
Eating a big breakfast made them full.

Try to reverse the apparent clauses.

Is dangerous driving too fast.
(Is dangerous, driving too fast.)

The students know that this is not an English sentence. In these examples, the students have turned the incomplete clause into a group of words that function like a noun.

Speeding *is dangerous.*
Going fast *is dangerous.*

__Driving too fast__ is dangerous.
__Driving a powerful car too fast__ is dangerous.
(__Driving the car that belongs to his friend__ is dangerous.)

The above groups or phrases are known as noun groups, because each one functions as a noun, as the subject of the sentence, and as the subject of the verb *is*. They are not clauses. (However, the last example has been provided for you as teacher to show how an adjectival clause can be embedded inside a noun group; e.g. "that belongs to his friend".)

Adjectival clauses (See Pronouns p. 167)

Punctuation of clauses: comma

The comma acts as a marker within a sentence. Commas should be used sparingly to assist clarity of meaning and to avoid ambiguity.

One-clause or simple sentences do not require commas, unless they contain a list of items.

Pattern: Independent clause.

The car rolled down the hill.

Commas are used:
- before a coordinating conjunction in compound sentences where each independent clause has a different topic or subject.

Pattern: Independent clause, + independent clause.

Coffee and tea were served, but there was no cake.
We have hidden the chocolates, and it is your task to find them.
   independent clause   independent clause

Commas are used:
- between each long clause in a sentence

Pattern: Long clause, + long clause.

We had been on the beach for many hours that day, and (we) decided that it was time to find shelter.
   long clause   long clause

Note:
Although the independent clauses have the same subject, the amount of information carried in the first clause warrants the use of the comma.

Commas are used:
- after an introductory dependent clause (periodic sentence)

Pattern: Dependent clause, + independent clause.

As there were few sales, the item was taken off the market.
   dependent clause   independent clause

Note:
There is no comma when the independent clause is placed first in the sentence (loose sentence).

The item was taken off the market as there were few sales.
   independent clause   dependent clause

Commas are used:
- when a sentence begins with an introductory adverb

Pattern: Adverb, independent clause.

Quickly, he drew the child into his arms.
  adverb   independent clause

Commas are used:
- at the beginning and end of restricted adjectival clauses (also known as clauses in apposition) which provide more details

Pattern: Subject (of independent clause), adjectival clause, rest of independent clause.

John Brown, who used to be at school with me, is now living in Perth.
subject   adjectival clause   independent clause

Note:
The adjectival clause is part of the noun group which includes the subject.

Commas are used:
- in sentences which begin with an introductory phrase

Pattern: Phrase, independent clause.

Towards the end of the road, a large sign warned motorists of the danger ahead
phrase   independent clause

Commas are used:
- in sentences which list a series of items

Pattern: Topic and first part of comment, word, word(,) + word.

Our garden had geraniums, roses, pansies, camellias and impatiens.

Note:
There is no comma, *and*. (Except in the US.)

Commas are used:
- to separate more than one adjective used before a noun

Pattern: Adjective, adjective topic + comment.

Fit, highly-trained players are required for this match.
adjective   adjective

Commas are used:
- after salutations and vocatives which do not end a sentence

Dear Madam,
John, you are not allowed to play in the rain.

Commas are used:
- in direct speech

Pattern 1: "Clause," they said.

"It's all snow and ice," she said.

Pattern 2: They said, "clause".

She said, "I am not going with you."

Pattern 3: "First part of clause," they said, "rest of clause."

"That's my car," he said, "when I win the lottery."

Commas are not used between short independent **clauses with the same subject** linked by coordinating conjunctions such as *and, but, or*.

Pattern: Independent clause + independent clause

*The dog barked loudly and **(the dog)** growled menacingly.*
*They were tired but **(they)** felt they could go on.*
     independent clause   independent clause

Commas should **not** be used:
- after abbreviations such as: e.g. i.e. viz.
- between State name and postcode: Queensland 4034
- after house numbers in an address: 59 Newcastle Street
- in dates: 10 June 1908
- at the end of each line of an address:
  The Premier of New South Wales
  Parliament House
  Sydney NSW 2000

CONJUNCTIONS (JOINING WORDS)

Conjunctions are words used to join clauses, groups of words and words. Conjunctions show relationships between the clauses of a sentence (written language) or utterance (spoken language).

Coordinating conjunctions	Relationship
and	additive
but	adversative
or	alternative
yet, however	limiting

Subordinating conjunctions	Relationship
because, as, since	cause/effect time
when, as, while, before, after, until	time
as soon as, since	time
if, unless, whether	condition
in order that, so that	purpose, reason
though, although, however	limiting

where, wherever   place
as if, though, although   concession

Correlative conjunctions are conjunctions which pair together to show closer links or relationships between ideas. The most common are:

both ... and
not only ... but also
either ... or
neither ... nor
whether ... or

Correlative conjunctions are used so that the same construction after each part is maintained;

e.g.

1. Both children and their parents may go.

2. Not only the sun by day but also the moon by night will light up this journey.

3. Whether he decides to go or she decides to stay, I am leaving.

NOUNS

The name or word for any person, thing, place, idea or feeling is a **noun**. Nouns are classified in a variety of ways, and have features such as number.

Proper nouns

Proper nouns are the names of people, places, days and months, and are usually written with a capital letter. Examples are:

John   Guinevere   Sydney   Monday   October   Australia

Common nouns

Examples are:

dog   chair   person   car

Abstract nouns

Abstract nouns name concepts, ideas and feelings. Examples are:

fear   happiness   danger

Collective nouns (See also p. 54)

Collective nouns name groups of things. Examples are:

crew   team   herd   congregation

There are subcategories of collective nouns:

specific	*army class club committee crew gang*
generic	*the public the clergy the media*
unique	*the Commonwealth of Australia the United Nations*
mass	*much food more food less food*
count	*many potatoes more potatoes fewer potatoes*
measure	*a loaf of bread litres of milk a piece of information*

Nouns and gender

Although contemporary English does not rely upon words which differentiate between genders, it is still useful to know **feminine** and **masculine** nouns which students will encounter in their reading. However, most feminine forms made by adding *'-ess'* are no longer used, and the original form (*actor, aviator, steward* and *priest*) is used.

ACTIVITIES

These activities can be undertaken with students in small groups or in whole-class groups.

One

Ask each student to list five favourite foods. Write these words on large sheets of paper as students read out their lists. Tell the students that this list is a list of nouns. Then classify the words (foods) into vegetables, fruits, cereals, etc. List the words divided into their categories on charts and display the charts.

Two

Over a period of days, the students can add new items to the categories, and check these entries for meaning and spelling.

Three

Group the students in fours and ask each group to use an atlas to list rivers, oceans, capital cities, Asian countries, towns in Australia and so on. Allocate one list to each group. After five minutes, ask group leaders to report, copying their lists onto large sheets of paper and displaying these. When all the lists have been put up, ask the students to find five more items for each list. Talk about these nouns and add some to the lists displayed.

Four

Ask the students to list boys' names, girls' names, games (one word only), heroes, ideas and feelings.

Five

Ask students to build sentences by replacing the nouns in the following sentences:

Mary gave a book to Tom in China.
Last year the football tournament was played in Sydney.

Six

Other lists of nouns can be generated. One of the most useful ways of listing groups of nouns is alphabetically, and these lists can then be used in other activities. The students can make an alphabetical list of people's names, animals, cities and musical instruments. Some lists will necessarily be incomplete.

Note:
The alphabetical list of animal names will be used later in several activities.

Seven

Lists of nouns can be generated for the following categories:
- names of persons in your family
- names of classmates
- names of places you have been
- names of countries you would like to visit one day
- names of important people in your life
- names of feelings you have when you are going to a party
- names of feelings you have during a bad day
- important inventions
- scientific ideas
- important behaviours (honesty, friendliness, etc.).

Punctuation: apostrophes

Apostrophes signal possession

> *the girl's bag (= the bag of the girl)* one girl
> *the girls' bags (= the bags of the girls)* more than one girl

Use the three-step way to form possessives:
1. Write the base word   *boy*
2. Add the apostrophe after the word   *boy'*
3. If there is no *s*, add one   *boy's*

Examples are given below.

Possessive singulars

base word	*man*
plus apostrophe	*man'*
plus s	*man's*

base word	*Mary*
plus apostrophe	*Mary'*
plus s	*Mary's*

dog's   cat's   woman's   child's   man's

Possessive plurals

Possession by plural nouns is shown by an apostrophe after the *s*.

| base word | *teachers* |
| plus apostrophe | *teachers'* |

| base word | *travel agents* |
| plus apostrophe | *travel agents'* |

boys'   dogs'   cats'   companions'

the machines' parts
the Smiths' car
the players' room
ladies' dresses

Indefinite pronouns

base word	*someone*
plus apostrophe	*someone'*
plus s	*someone's*

base word	*no one*
plus apostrophe	*no one'*
plus s	*no one's*

one's   somebody's   everybody's   another's   anyone's

Animate nouns

a person's legs   a horse's mouth

Note the following **plural nouns**: (the noun is already plural)

*people's vote   women's hostel   men's club
oxen's plough   sheep's fleece*

Singular nouns ending in s (sibilant sound /s/)

In words of two or more syllables, and which end with sibilant sounds such as *Jesus*, *Odysseus*, *the masses*, *princess* (singular), *princesses* (plural), *princes* (plural), *Rameses*, an apostrophe is added without an *s* to avoid three sibilant sounds (sss).

*Jesus'   Odysseus'   the masses'   princess'   princesses'
princes'   Rameses'*

Note:
Apostrophes are also used in expression of time such as *one month's leave* (leave of one month) and *a day's work* (work of one day) but they are now increasingly omitted from these expressions when they are written in the plural form: *in twelve years time, ten months suspension, three months holiday, six hours start,* as the words are seen as compound nouns used in an adjectival sense.

Apostrophes are used to show joint ownership as follows:

>*my uncle and aunt's holiday*
>*my brother and sister's trip*

Note:
In *Maughan's and Huxley's writings* each has an apostrophe, indicating two separate sets of writings, not one joint set.

Plural nouns do **not** have an apostrophe *s*. For example:

>*videos   tomatoes   potatoes   cigarettes*
>*pizzas   DVDs   CDs*

Possessive pronouns

These pronouns do not take an apostrophe.

>its   hers   his   their   ours   yours

This sweater is hers
Are these books yours?

Apostrophe of omission

Apostrophes also signal that one or more letters is missing in a word. A word using the apostrophe is called a contraction. For example: *I am — I'm, you are — you're, cannot — can't, it is — it's.*

VERBS

Verbs are often known as 'doing words', but verbs are also 'being words' (*is, am, were* ...) and 'having words'. The verb expresses the action that is being performed; it is needed in a clause. Verbs are classified in a number of ways according to function: **tense**, **voice** and **mood**. Verbs may also be classified in other ways, such as whether they are **transitive** or **intransitive**, and **regular** or **irregular**. Verbs take **participial** forms in present and past tense, and have an **infinitive** form.

Tense

The tense of the verb shows one or more of a number of functions. Tense is often said to refer to time. The tense used is an indication of the **present** (*I write*), **past** (*I wrote*) and **future** (*I will write*).

The description above is only partly true. Tense is also used to indicate continuation and/or completion. For example:

> *The girl wanted to go to the dance.* (and maybe still wants to)

The verb *wanted* is in the past tense, but within the meaning of the expression can refer to an event that is yet to occur.

The common tenses of the verb are shown in the following:

*I **said** that he **will want** that car. He **says** it all the time.*
past tense   future tense   present tense

There are a number of other tenses such as perfect, past perfect, and the continuous past, present and future tenses. Some of these tenses involve the use of participles:

*I am **going** to the place where they had **gone**.*
present participle   past participle

Verbs also occur in the infinitive form:

*I want **to stay**.*
infinitive

Voice

This function of verbs is concerned with the relationship between the verb and its subject and object. For example, we can write:

The dog bit the man.
active voice

The man was bitten by the dog.
passive voice

These examples clearly have the same meaning: *The dog bit the man.* The same thing can be said using the passive voice, where the subject and object change position. That is, the subject moves into the predicate and part of the predicate becomes the subject. There is, in the above example, a change in the verb from past tense to the use of *was* together with the past participle *bitten*.

To state all of this another way, the dog performs the action on the man. The agent of action affects the object of action. This is called active voice.

Passive voice is used when the object of the action (as subject) is acted upon by the agent of action.

The use of the passive voice requires the use of one of the helping verbs of the verb *to be* with a participle.

*I **ran** the mile distance.*
active voice

*The mile distance **was run** by me.*
passive voice

Mood

The term mood is used to indicate the varieties of expression that reflect manner or intent. There are four moods:

The lady went to the shops.
indicative mood

Did the lady go to the shops?
interrogative mood

Go to the shops!
imperative mood

If I were able to go to the shops, I would.
subjunctive mood (wish or modal)

The indicative mood is used for a **statement** or **declaration**.

The interrogative mood is used for a **question** (and is sometimes regarded as part of the declarative mood).

The imperative mood is used for an **order** or command.

The subjunctive mood expresses a **wish**, a possibility, or imagining.

The subjunctive mood is marked for special treatment as there are specific words that can indicate its use. These are known as **modal auxiliary verbs**: *can, could, may, might, shall, should, will, would, must.*

Note:
The use of *will* and *shall* in the future tense does not necessarily show the subjunctive mood but usually expresses the indicative mood.

> *If it was my choice, I will say yes* (statement)
> *If it were my choice, I would say yes* (subjunctive)

Transitive and intransitive verbs

Transitive verbs take a **direct object**.

> *I read **the book***
> (direct object)

Intransitive verbs take an **indirect object**.

> ***Susan** smiled **at me.***
> (indirect object indicated by preposition)

Clauses can incorporate transitive verbs that take both a direct and indirect object.

> *I gave the book* (direct object) *to her* (indirect object).
> *I gave her* (indirect object) *the book* (direct object).

Note:
There are instances of intransitive verbs taking a direct object, for example, *She smiled bouquets.* (This may have something to do with the fact that users of English bend the 'rules' according to dialect or

style or both.) English dictionaries show whether particular verbs are transitive or intransitive (or both), by showing *vt* or *vi* at the beginning of the entry for the word.

Regular and irregular verbs

Most verbs change form according to some general rule. For example, the change into participial forms is made by adding *-ing* (present participle), and *-ed* (past participle), as in the following regular (or weak) verbs:

	present participle	past participle	past tense
walk	**walking**	**walked**	**walked**
depend	**depending**	**depended**	**depended**
receive	**receiving**	**received**	**received**

There are a number of irregular verbs which do not follow the rule above, as with the following verbs:

	present participle	past participle	past tense
give	**giving**	**given**	**gave**
done	**did**	**do**	**done**

The past tense and past participial forms of more irregular verbs are listed in the Table of verbs on page 151.

ACTIVITIES

One

Select a verb of action such as *walk, sail,* or *make*. Ask groups of students to list as many words as they can that mean the same as the verb selected. Students will need to use a thesaurus for this activity. For example, the list for *walk* is:

amble foot march trot pace saunter parade promenade sidle strut stroll stride toddle tramp waddle trundle perambulate mince sashay limp hobble shuffle stagger stumble totter plod clump lumber slog traipse trample

Ask students to use their dictionaries to find the meaning of each word. Where necessary, ask students to act out styles of walking, then choose the words which best describe them. Write each word on a card and place the cards in a word bank or list them on a wall chart.

Two

Match each of the words for walk to the alphabetical list of animals. For example, *aardvarks amble, bears trundle, elephants tramp*. This will work best if you use the plural nouns from the list.

List the word pairs. These could be written in a pad and illustrated by the students to produce a book of *Ark Walks*.

Three

Ask students to complete the following sequences:

present	past	future	past perfect
walk	walked	will walk	had walked
throw	threw	will throw	had thrown
give			had given
	did		
		will be	
			had gone

(Use the Table of verbs and a dictionary to help.)

Table of verbs

	Tense		Participle	
	present	*past*	*present*	*present*
action (doing)	walk	walked	walking	walked
	give	gave	giving	given
	throw	threw	throwing	thrown
	come	came	coming	come
	go	went	going	gone
	do	did	doing	done
	run	ran	running	run
	catch	caught	catching	caught
	bring	brought	bringing	brought
	depend	depended	depending	depended
	receive	received	receiving	received
	sneak	sneaked	sneaking	sneaked
	buy	bought	buying	bought
	bend	bent	bending	bent
	bleed	bled	bleeding	bled
saying	talk	talked	talking	talked
	tell	told	telling	told
	say	said	saying	said
	describe	described	describing	described
perceiving, thinking, feeling	see	saw	seeing	seen
	think	thought	thinking	thought
	feel	felt	feeling	felt
	know	knew	knowing	known
	appear	appeared	appearing	appeared
	learn	learned	learning	learned
		learnt		learnt
	teach	taught	teaching	taught
having	have	had	having	had
being	am/are	was/were	being	been

Four

Ask the students to use a thesaurus to find synonyms for **said** in the following passage.

Mary Smith said that it was a nice day and said could she visit her friend. Her mother said that she could, and also said that the girls were not to go too far along the bush track.

Many hours later Mrs Smith said it was getting late and that the girls had not returned. She said that someone should go and look for them. A few minutes later she said she was worried but Mr Smith said not to worry yet. He said that it was not dark.

Just as night began to fall, Mr Smith said that he had better go and look for the girls when they appeared. Mrs Smith said that the girls were late, and said that she had been worried about them. She sounded a little angry and upset.

The girls said that they were sorry.

These words will help:

*utter sound voice recite intone dictate
deliver mention name comment allow
express observe quote remark state
harangue harp preach exclaim gasp chatter
babble blab snap snarl spit whine grumble
whisper breathe murmur sigh
shout yell drawl croak drone reflect
talk interject question phrase quip boast
brag bluster rant enunciate pronounce
vocalise stress speak articulate gossip
stammer stutter quaver splutter mutter
mumble gabble lisp*

Give the students opportunities to change more words than *said*. Allow them to work in small groups, as there is much they can learn from each other as they discuss the meanings of the words chosen. Encourage students to provide examples of their writing for verb substitution. With permission from the students, photocopy the writing and use it for more work on verb substitution.

Five

Ask a student to retell a story from a wall chart or fable and write down what is said. Check that the verbs used by the student are all in the same tense as the original, and that the correct tenses have been maintained throughout the retelling. With the retold story on a screen or whiteboard, ask the students to compare the use of verbs in the original and the retold versions.

Also consider the student's choice of words, and discuss how well the choices fit, and their suitability.

Six

Encourage students to develop their grammar and vocabulary through word substitution and expansion of sentences.

> *The hare ran faster than ever before.*
> *The desperate hare raced faster than ever.*
> *The hare was so desperate that it ran faster then ever before in order to catch the tortoise before the race finished.*

ADJECTIVES (DESCRIBING WORDS)

Adjectives are used to describe, add detail and give finer meaning to the noun. There are many types of adjectives, and it is not possible to say that a word is an adjective by looking at it in isolation from the words that surround it. There are a few suffixes, such as *-ful, -less* and *-ous* that give a clue to identifying adjectives: *beautiful, careless, dangerous*. However, the function rather than its form determines an adjective.

Descriptive adjectives are used to state some quality of the noun.

>*a **friendly** dog   an **interesting** book   an **old** person*

Quantitative adjectives tell how much of something is meant; e.g. *half, daily, weekly, fourfold, full, whole, part, little, much, any, some, no, enough, all, sufficient.*

>**some** *person*   **much** *happiness*   **little** *joy*

Numerical adjectives are numbers, both cardinal and ordinal.

one   first   twenty   thirteenth

Multiple adjectives state quantity or number.

double   triple   dozen   few   numerous   several   some   many

Demonstrative adjectives show which noun is being talked about; e.g. *this, that, these, those.*

***this** hat   **those** wigs*

Distributive adjectives are used with nouns that can be referred to separately or in groups; e.g. *each, neither, either, only.*

***each** person   **either** car   **only** child*

Inflection of adjectives

Adjectives inflect for degree: **positive**, **comparative** or **superlative**. The comparative and superlative are usually formed by the addition of *-er* and *-est* to the positive form. In some instances, *more* and *most* are placed before the positive form. The two systems for forming the comparative and superlative forms are not used together. There are a few irregular adjectives.

The **positive** degree is the usual form of the adjective; e.g. *sweet, good, beautiful.*

The **comparative** degree is used to make a comparison between two items; e.g. *sweeter, better, more beautiful.* The comparative is followed by *than*.

*Honey is **sweeter than** an orange.*

The superlative degree is used when more than two items are compared; e.g. *sweetest, best, most beautiful*. The superlative is usually followed by a preposition, such as *of, among, in*.

He is the **oldest of** *the three.*

Inflecting adjectives by adding *-er* and *-est* to the adjective applies to adjectives which consist of one or two syllables. If the adjective has three syllables, then *more or most* is placed before the adjective.

positive form	comparative form	superlative form
old	*older*	*oldest*
new	*newer*	*newest*
pretty	*prettier*	*prettiest*
expensive	*more expensive*	*most expensive*
beautiful	*more beautiful*	*most beautiful*

Sometimes the 'rough and ready' rule about the number of syllables does not apply. The word *handsome*, for example, uses *more* and *most* rather than the inflected endings *-er* and *-est*.

There are some adjectives which change entirely to form the comparative and the superlative forms:

positive form	comparative form	superlative form
good	*better*	*best*
bad	*worse*	*worst*
little	*less*	*least*
many	*more*	*most*
much	*more*	*most*

Note:
There is a tendency in some varieties of English to use *littler* and *littlest* Encourage students to use *smaller* and *smallest* unless there is a stylistic purpose for choosing *littler* and *littlest*.

ACTIVITIES

There is little point in working with adjectives and nouns separately. Using the two parts of speech together is what occurs naturally in spoken language, and the functions of the adjective are more easily displayed for the students to see and discuss if they are paired with nouns.

One

Obtain two small boxes and many small cards, about 5 cm x 2 cm in size. Half of the cards should be one colour, say white. The other half should be another colour, say green. Write as many adjectives as you can on the green cards, one word per card. Put these words in one of the boxes. Write the same number of nouns on the white cards, but ensure that these nouns are suitable for the adjectives you have chosen to use. Place the white cards in the other box.

BOX 1
brown fluffy hairy green spotted dangerous smooth rough gentle friendly hostile warm cold black striped loud quiet

BOX 2
lion cat panther leopard puma cheetah cougar jaguar tiger ocelot tortoiseshell Persian Siamese Manx

You can use any nouns; there is no need to group the nouns in this manner.

Put the students into groups of four or five. (You will need two boxes for each group.) Ask the students to draw a card from each box. Each student talks about her or his pair of words. The students can trade one of their cards and discuss the new pair of noun and adjective. Introduce the word **adjective** as a general term to use for the words on the green cards. The students can talk about the effect that these words have on the nouns. Finish the activity by listing adjective-noun pairs on paper for all the students to see and use in their writing.

Two

Read the story *Brown Bear Brown Bear* by Bill Martin. This story uses colours for each of a number of animals. The students can substitute other colours and shapes, numbers and texture words for the adjectives in the original story.

> *I see a striped cow looking at me.*
> *I see two spotted green dogs looking at me.*

The students can write their own words on cards and place these over the adjectives in the original text. They can write their own stories and illustrate these. Continue to use the term adjective with ease and naturally as part of your discussion about the students' choices of words to describe the animals in the story.

Three

Use dictionaries, encyclopedias and thesauruses. Ask the students to go back to the alphabetical list of animals which was made earlier and give each animal one or more adjectives that start with the same letter as the animal's name does. For example:

> *ancient adventurous ambling anxious aardvarks*
> *brown bumbling beautiful bouncing brave bears*

The students can take these lists and create stories, drawings and friezes of their creations.

Simile and metaphor

Adjectives are words that name **attributes**, and when an adjective is added to a noun it describes that word more fully. Students can also describe something in terms of what it is like, and this introduces another dimension to writing and speaking. The use of **simile** and **metaphor** enhances the image the writer tries to create in words, and is often more effective than using adjectives. A judicious use of adjective and simile can be useful.

See Teaching noun groups and expanded noun groups pp. 183–188.

Order of adjectives

There is an accepted order for two or more adjectives before a noun. Students whose first language is English have no difficulty with ordering the following: *Scottish, cold, three, players* into *three cold Scottish players*. Generally, the 'rule' is: number first, then place the adjectives in sequence from the more general to the more specific attribute.

ADVERBS

Adverbs are words that describe or give further information about verbs, adjectives and other adverbs. Adverbs therefore describe attributes of verbs and act as qualifiers or modifiers. The adverb functions in relation to the verb in much the same way that the adjective functions in relation to the noun.

The most common ending for adverbs is *-ly,* a suffix from Old English that means like. Adverbs can be formed from almost all adjectives by adding *-ly,* as in *anxiously, beautifully* and *easily*. However, there are a few adverbs that do not end in *-ly*: *fast, soon, more, less, now, then, here, there, far, near, often, never, seldom* are some examples. There are a number of adjectives that cannot take an *-ly* ending to make an adverb: *best, little, fast* are some examples.

Some examples of adverbs acting as modifiers include the following:

    *She drives **fast**.*
            adverb

He drives ***very*** ***slowly****.*
               adverb adverb

They drive ***very***   *old*   *cars.*
              adverb adjective   noun

The words *deep, long, hard, fast, early* and *longer* are examples of words that can function both as adjectives and adverbs. The function of the word determines what part of speech it is. However, it is easier to think of the adjectives and adverbs as acting as qualifiers, and not to attempt to classify each item unnecessarily.

Not all words that end in *-ly* are adverbs, either. *Homely, timely, manly* and *lovely* are words that end in *-ly* and which are used as adjectives; e.g. *timely arrival, lovely building.*

Comparison of adverbs

The general rule for comparison of adverbs is to use the word *more* as a qualifier before the adverb; e.g. *more quickly.*

There are few opportunities for using the superlative form of adverbs, although some speakers will say that a job was *finished most quickly.*

ACTIVITIES

One

Use two small boxes and a number of cards for each group of students. The cards could be 5 cm x 2 cm; half could be light brown and the other half light blue. Write one verb per card on the brown cards. Write adverbs on the blue cards.

Use a thesaurus to help you select words for verbs that are similar in meaning, or which can be classified according to some semantic category; e.g. WALK: *march, tread, step, pace, wend, promenade, trudge, tramp, stalk, stride, strut, toddle, trot, canter, gallop, prance, amble.*

For adverbs you could choose words that can be used with walking; e.g. QUICKLY: *speedily, swiftly, fleetly, rapidly, nimbly, agilely, expeditiously, expressly, actively, fast.* (You could add an extra adverb and its synonyms.)

You could also use antonyms to generate pairs. For example, SLOWLY: *tardily, easily, gently, slackly, deliberately, gradually, sensibly, languidly, sluggishly.*

Hint:
You will find it useful to look up the adjective in the thesaurus, and then add *-ly*.

Invite the students to select a card from the verb box and move or walk in the manner stated on the card. You will need to explain and even demonstrate some words for students. Then ask the students to select a card from the adverb box and change or modify their style of walking in order to show the new meaning. (This activity allows you to bring some movement into your classroom, and permits discussion of the nuances of meaning brought about by the selection of words and their use together. It allows opportunities for developing the extensive vocabulary necessary for reading and writing.)

Early in this lesson or activity, introduce and use the word adverb and use it regularly and naturally. It is much easier for you to ask the students to take words from the 'verb box' and the 'adverb box'.

Two

In this round of the Alphabet Animal Game the students will use all four open-class parts of speech. Ask the students to find words (nouns, adjectives, verbs and adverbs) to build up 'alphabet animal' clauses.

They may use dictionaries and encyclopedias, and may occasionally refer to a thesaurus to do this, as follows:
1. List the names of 26 animals, one for each letter of the alphabet. Insist that students use the plural form; e.g. *antelopes, bears, cats*.
2. Ask the students to find one word (an adjective that can tell us something about each animal. This adjective must begin with the same letter as the name of the animal; e.g. *alert antelopes, brown bears, cool cats*.
3. Ask the students to give the animal something to do by choosing a verb. The verb must begin with the same letter as the name of the animal; e.g. *alert antelopes act, brown bears bounce, cool cats climb*.
4. Ask the students to find a word (an adverb) that shows how the animal does this action; e.g.:

> *Alert antelopes act anxiously.*
> *Brown bears bounce beautifully.*
> *Cool cats climb carelessly.*

5. Ask the students to write their own four-word one clause sentence (simple sentence).

Hints:
Insist that students use the plural form of the noun and the present simple tense of the verb. Some students use the present participial form of the verb on its own, thus producing an incomplete clause.

This activity can be used later to alert students to agreement between noun and verb.

> *An alert antelope acts anxiously.*
> *Alert antelopes act anxiously.*

For your assistance:

> *Quiet quokkas quibble quietly.*
> *Xenophobic xemes xerox xylogenetically.*
> *Excellent foxes excavate excessively.*
> *Zany zebras zigzag zealously.*

Three

Ask students to put the most useful adverb in the most appropriate part of each sentence.

slowly   efficiently   cheerfully   today   fast

He walked along the road.
She ran down the street.

Discuss shifts in meaning that depend on where the adverb is placed.

Four

Ask the students to complete the following table:

heavy   **heavily**
bad
serious
reasonable
quiet
absolute
extreme
fast

Spelling adverbs

If the adjective ends in *-le*, drop the *e* before adding the *-y*.

reasonable   *reasonably*

If the adjective ends in *-e*, keep the *e* and add *-ly*.

polite   *politely*

PRONOUNS (REFERRING WORDS)

Pronouns are words that are used to refer to and substitute for one or more words or ideas. Pronouns are particularly important since they can refer to information in other sentences and in other parts of the text being read or spoken.

> *The old couple owned a dog that had won many prizes.* **They** *took* **it** *to shows everywhere.*

They refers to *the old couple*. *It* refers to *a dog that had won many prize*s.

Special features of pronouns

Some of the most important features of pronouns are **case**, **number**, **gender** and **reflexivity**. Pronouns have singular and plural forms. There is gender distinction in the third person singular forms, and this distinction is carried into the reflexive forms.

Pronouns in English are inflected to mark their case: **subjective**, **objective** and **possessive**. The case form is determined by the relationship of the pronoun to the other words in and between the clauses and sentences. The table shows the case forms of the English pronouns, as well as their reflexive forms.

There is a special group of pronouns called **relative pronouns**: *who*, *which* and *that*. *Who* also has case forms: *who, whom, whose*.

Finally, there is the indefinite pronoun *one*.

Pronouns have come to us from Old English, and are the only part of speech to remain inflected in a regular way. Pronouns also indicate the gender of the person or thing referred to, whether masculine (m), feminine (f), or neuter (n), shown in the case chart below. The gender distinction in English applies only to the singular. Plural pronouns do not indicate gender.

Case Chart of Pronouns

Subjective	**Possessive**	**Objective**	**Possessive**	**Reflexive Forms**
I	*my*	*me*	*mine*	*myself*
we	*our*	*us*	*ours*	*ourselves*
you	*your*	*you*	*yours*	*yourself*
you	*your*	*you*	*yours*	*yourselves*
he (m)	*his*	*him*	*his*	*himself*
she (f)	*her*	*her*	*hers*	*herself*
it (n)	*its*	*it*	*its*	*itself*
they	*their*	*them*	*theirs*	*themselves*
who	*whose*	*whom*	—	—

Relative pronouns and adjectival clauses

The **relative pronoun** is used as a form of conjunction to join a clause to the noun being described. This special clause is known as an **adjectival clause**. (In some theories of grammar, the term relative clause is used as the clause begins with a relative pronoun.)

*The old couple **who** lived down the road*
adjectival clause
*owned a dog **that barked often.***
adjectival clause

The independent clause is *The old couple owned a dog*. The adjectival clauses give details about the couple and their dog. From a functional grammar perspective, the verb *owned* functions as a process, and the participants on each side are noun groups that contain embedded adjectival clauses with embedded circumstances (*down the road* and *often*).

Pronouns

The ways in which pronouns are now used has created two sets of principles in recent decades.

Gender-neutral English is important, and modern writing requires that care be taken to respect this principle. The first way to meet this requirement is to write using plural nouns so that the required pronouns are *they, them, their* and *themselves*.

When a singular noun is used for people, the required pronoun is also *they, them* and *their*. For example, *That person has forgotten their belongings*. Sometimes, writers can create problems when the referring function of pronouns is confused by poor writing. For example, here is a sentence written in a daily newspaper some years ago.

A man was badly injured in a road accident at Bellyband Road and had to be helped by paramedics. They were taken to hospital and is in a stable condition.

Pronouns function as referring words, and obviously the writer's determination to avoid using *he* or *she* has created the problem. Thinking about the second sentence alerts the listener to the fact that the *man* is in a stable condition, not the *paramedics*. But the problem could have been avoided if that writer had realised that the gender had already been established: *man*. But what would happen if the writer had said a *driver*? Again, *they* is still a problem. The writer would need to use the noun again rather than use a pronoun to refer to that noun; that is, *The driver was taken to hospital and is in a stable condition.*

There is a second principle for the use of pronouns:

Inclusive language

Inclusive language is a principle whereby no person is left unacknowledged and disrespected in all social, workplace and other contexts. LGBTIQ people have been particularly marginalised, and society is now changing to becoming more inclusive of all people. In order to recognise someone and to respond appropriately, there are a few guidelines:

1. Accept how individuals define their gender and sexuality.
   When informed by an individual about their sexuality or gender, use the terms that individual uses to describe themselves.
2. Use language that encompasses all groups, terms such as *partner, everybody, folks.*
3. There are increasingly more people who wish selected pronouns to be used in reference to them. If you need to know, ask the person if you may ask which pronoun they use.
4. Keep in mind that some individuals wish their pronoun use to be specific to context and not widely used.

For more information, visit LGBTIQ+ Inclusive Language Guide | Victorian Government at https://www.vic.gov.au/inclusive-language-guide

ACTIVITIES

One

Ask the students to read the following paragraph and replace some of the words with other words that will avoid their repetition. Discuss individual responses. Write the pronouns in red on or under the words that have been replaced.

Mary and John went for a picnic.
Mary and John *took the dog called Rufus.*
She and he/They

Rufus *was a fine dog.* ***Rufus*** *had*
He/It   He/It
won many pins at the local Dog Show.

Some other examples you can use in replacing subject nouns with pronouns:

Carlo *went to the film.* ***Carlo*** *was happy.*
Maria *plays football.* ***Maria*** *is captain of the team.*
Paula *collects toy cars and dolls.* ***Paula*** *has many cars and dolls.*
Mark and Mary *went to the beach.* ***Mark and Mary*** *had a great day.*

Two

List common pronouns on the board or on paper. Encourage students to help you to write a short paragraph that makes use of these pronouns naturally.

Discuss the words that are replaced by the pronouns. You may wish to:
a. Have a number of short paragraphs ready for the purpose.
b. Use examples from students' writing. (Obtain permission from the students whose writing is used.)

c. Ask students to work in groups on examples provided from photocopied worksheets.
d. Display a Pronouns Chart in your classroom. (The detail will vary according to the age of the students you are working with.)

Three

Develop pattern sentences using pronouns. For example:

The boy rode _____ bike.
Possessive: my, our, your, his, her, its, their

The old man saw _____ at the show.
Objective: me, us, you, him, her, it, them

_____ like eating ice-cream.
Subjective: I, we, you, he, she, it, they

The stolen car was _____.
Possessive: mine, ours, yours, his, hers, its, theirs

Four

Develop pattern sentences using reflexive pronouns instead of the subjective case. For example:

I gave the present to _____.
We gave the present to _____.
You gave the present to _____. (singular)
You gave the present to _____. (plural)
He gave the present to _____.
She gave the present to _____.
It gave the present to _____.
They gave the present to _____. (themselves)

Note: Reflexive means 'to self'.

Five

Ask the students to rewrite paragraphs using pronouns. For example:

> *The dog that lives next door barks at my cat all the time. One day the gate next door was open and it got out and ran after my cat. My cat stopped and glared at it and then it ran away.*

Ask students to discuss the problems caused by inappropriate use and overuse of pronouns. Use the following paragraph as an example:

Too Many Pronouns (A Fable)

I said to him that she had said to her that its name was too long for them to remember and that we could help our friends who wanted to come if he sent his car to their place first and then to mine and yours. You know whose place it went to first and sent us looking for those for whom one had waited. This took you to her place and theirs. They were sorry this had not been to ours and that to hers so we sent these back.

In the paragraph above, all pronouns except reflexive pronouns have been used. Note that the words *this, that* and *those* have been included. They function as pronouns.

This, that, these, those

These words are known by a variety of terms. They are called **demonstratives**, **adjectives** and **pronouns**. Some grammarians even give them a double name such as **demonstrative adjective** (***this*** car), or **demonstrative pronoun.** (*Give **this** to them.*) When demonstratives function as words that refer to other words in a text, they have to be given the same care as pronouns.

Reference to events outside the text

The word *it* is often used to refer to some outside event in such expressions as: *It is a nice day* and *It has been said that ...* Such uses of *it* are normal in varieties of spoken English, but need to be used with care in written English.

PREPOSITIONS (POSITION WORDS)

Prepositions are parts of speech that show relationships expressed in terms of time and space.

*The dog carried the bone **at** night to the corner **of** the room **without** a fuss.*

There are a limited number of prepositions in English, but they are pervasive. Prepositions can be single words or phrases. Prepositions can be arranged as follows:

Place
in   out   into   out of   inside   outside
on   off   onto   upon
to   from
up   down
over   under   above   below
beside   beneath   before   behind   beyond
with   witbout   within
at   near   by   past   after   next to   in front of

*along around across against
through throughbout
amid among between
of for except*

Time
*before after during
at by
since till until
in on*

There are a number of expressions that function as prepositions, and bring other meanings besides time and place to prepositional phrases. Some examples are: **with regard** to that matter, **because of** his temper, **according to** Hoyle.

There are a few examples of present participial forms of verbs functioning as prepositions:

*notwithstanding concerning
regarding respecting*
(*about* can be used in place of the last three)

ACTIVITIES

One

Write a couple of prepositions, such as *in, under, through, behind,* on the paper attached to your easel or on the whiteboard. Ask students to describe or show what these words indicate. The students need to be aware that these words show the position of something in relation to another thing. Write these relationships on the paper in the form of prepositional phrases, such as *under the tree, over the bridge, on the table.*

Ask the students for more prepositions and list these down the left side of the whiteboard or the page on your easel. Invite the students to use some of the prepositions in phrases, as shown above.

Organise the students into groups of three, and give each group a large sheet of paper and a felt pen. Tell them that each group is to produce its own poem following these rules:
1. Each line must begin with a preposition.
2. Prepositions that contain more than one word (e.g. *in front of, next to*) count as a single word.
3. Each line must have only two or three words.
4. The last line may contain as many words as you want.

Provide a model before the students begin. For example:
down the road
around the corner
near the bridge
before lunch
there was a very old person sitting in the sun.

Better still, develop a poem with the students. Give each group ten minutes to write the longest poem that they can compose in that time.

As the students work on their poems, move around and give encouragement and advice where required. When the students have finished, ask one student from each group to read that group's poem and place it on the easel for all to see as it is read to them. The groups can rewrite and illustrate their poems if they wish.

Talk about the patterns of language shown in the poem, pointing out that the word that begins each line is a preposition. The phrase that is produced for each line is a **prepositional phrase**.

There are older terms for this prepositional phrase pattern. They can be **adverbial phrases** if they function as adverbs. However, it is easier to use the form name (prepositional phrase) than the functional one. In functional grammar these phrases are examples of **circumstances**.

Two

It is a relatively simple exercise to build new texts on the structure of children's books; e.g.:

Bears in the Night by Stan and Jan Berenstain

Three

Using the book *My Cat Likes to Hide in Boxes* by Eve Sutton, ask the students to tell where the cat could hide in relation to the box. The cat could be:

> *behind the box*
> *beside the box*
> *near the box*
> *next to the box*
> *in the corner of the box*
> *on the box*
> *under the box*

The students could produce and illustrate a classroom book around this theme. Remember to keep each prepositional phrase on a page of its own or in a discrete position in relation to other phrases.

DETERMINERS (POINTING WORDS)

Some people say that this part of speech is a kind of grab-bag of the remaining grammatical words in English, but linguists have grouped them as determiners because they point to and determine how words function.

Articles: there are two types:

definite article *the*

The definite article points to or determines or defines what is being talked about; e.g.

The dog is eating **the** bone.

indefinite article *a (an* before a vowel or non-aspirated |h|)

The indefinite article points to or determines what is being talked about but is not defining.

***A** dog was eating **an** octopus for **an** hour.*

Possessives: (otherwise known as possessive pronouns or referring words)

my, your, our, his, her, its, their

Possessives determine which noun or object is owned. ***Their*** actions.

Relatives: (also known as relative pronouns) *who, whom, whose, which, that*

Relative pronouns are used to connect an adjectival clause to its related noun, the noun that precedes it. The relative pronoun determines or points to the noun that is being described by the adjectival clause.

*This was the book **that** I read last week.*
*It was his sister **who** scored the winning goal.*
*The police found the person **whose** pet had been lost.*

Interrogatives: *what, which, who, when, where, whose, how*

Interrogatives are words used at the beginning of questions.

***Where** is Dad going with that hatchet?*
***Who** did this?*

Negatives: *no, not*

Point to what is not agreed with.

Quantitatives: *some, any, enough, every, each, either, neither*

These words point to and determine the quantity of the noun or idea to which they point.

> ***Some** people are coming to visit.*
> ***Any** idea that you offer is welcome.*
> ***Each** is to be used and **every** other is to be left alone.*
> ***Either** is sufficiently useful in this task.*

Demonstratives: *this that these those*

These four words point to other words or ideas in the clause. There are two types of demonstratives:

Demonstrative adjectives, where the noun pointed to is placed next to it.

> ***This** book is the best on **that** topic.*
> ***These** ideas will not be well received by **those** people.*

Demonstrative pronouns, which refer to a noun or idea elsewhere in the text.

> ***This** can be seen clearly by analysing the mixture.*

Note:

Demonstrative pronouns are widely used by many writers at the beginning of paragraphs, and the referent is somewhere in the preceding paragraph. If that referent is not at the end of the paragraph, and is obliterated by too much other information, readers will not immediately make the connection between the demonstrative pronoun and its intended referent.

TEACHING NOUN GROUPS AND EXPANDED NOUN GROUPS

Presented below is a step-by-step procedure for teaching the following:
- Adjective-noun as a noun group
- Simple sentence (noun group + verb + prepositional phrase)
- Adjectival phrase
- Adjectival clause
- The difference between a phrase and a clause
- Why the clause always has a verb (because that is how it is!)
- Expanded noun groups
- Dependent clauses
- Simile (used as a phrase or as a clause)
- Embedded clauses
- Sentence
- And loads of metalanguage that students understand and can use.

Note:

If you teach this entire set of minilessons in one session, follow up with the steps being taught again, a part at a time. The students will be expected to show the use of each phrase, clause, noun group and simile in their daily writing, often with a reminder to add information to their text using one of these syntactic patterns.

You will need:

- Strips of coloured paper. All strips 4 cm wide.
- Use A4: short side for phrases, long side for clauses.
- A4 measures 21 cm x 30 cm
- Red (10 cm x 4 cm) for a noun
- Pink (21 cm x 4 cm) for an adjectival phrase
- Pink (30 cm x 4 cm) for adjectival clause
  (NB: **Have another five strips ready**)
- Green (10 cm x 4 cm) for a verb
- Blue (21 cm x 4 cm) for a prepositional phrase to go after the verb.

Optional for this lesson
- Blue (21cm x 4 cm) for simile written as a *like phrase*
- Blue (30 cm x 4 cm) for simile written as an as *if clause*

Lesson steps:

1. Students hold up red strip, as you do, and ask them to write the name of an animal on that strip. Insist that the animals have an "s" to signify the plural.

2. Students hold up the shortest pink strip, as you do, and ask them to write an adjective to describe their animals. Insist on a capital letter for their adjective as they will be writing a sentence.

3. Place your strips on the board: *Fabulous cheetahs*

4. Ask students which of those two words is the more important word (If necessary, cover each word in turn.)

   Ask why *cheetahs* (the noun) is more important, looking for the students to tell you that *cheetahs* is what the developing story is about. Tell them the *cheetahs* are the things we are talking about and is the **subject** of the sentence we are going to write.

5. Demonstrate completion of the sentence using the red and blue strips:

   Fabulous cheetahs speed across the grasslands.

         pink   red   green   ◀----- blue -------▶

   (You could tell students that the part of the sentence from the verb on is the **predicate**, the rest of the sentence or clause.)

6. Students read your sentence. Ask a number of students to read their sentences. Check that all students have this simple sentence structure above.

7. Talk about a simple sentence: one verb, one clause.

8. Make a space between the noun and the verb (cheetahs and speed).

9. Show and ask students to take the pink strip (21 cm x 4 cm) and write a **with phrase** on that strip to tell more about their animals; to describe their animals in a different way. (A **with phrase** is a phrase starting with the word ***with***.)

   *Fabulous cheetahs **with long legs** speed across the grasslands.*

10. Your developing noun group (in pink and red) and sentence is always on display as a model for your students to follow.

11. Point to the word *fabulous* and ask what kind of word it is, and what its function is; what it does. Elicit the statement that fabulous describes and is therefore a ***describing word***. Then ask for the proper name for a describing word: **adjective**.

12. Point to the 'with phrase' (*with long legs*) and ask what kind of phrase it is? What is its function? What does this phrase do? Elicit the statement that *with long legs* describes the *cheetahs* and is therefore a ***describing phrase***. Then ask for the proper name of a describing phrase: **adjectival phrase**.

13. Tell students that their noun group is a little bigger as we have added a phrase to it. Ask selected students to read their noun groups (*Fabulous cheetahs with long legs*).

14. Ask students what is the main noun in their noun group (cheetahs), and why it is the main noun (it *tells us what our story is about*; cheetahs is the subject of our story or sentence.) Note: Each student provides examples from their own noun group.

15. Ask students if there are any other nouns in their noun group. There will be a second one, but it is not the main noun or subject.
16. Make a space after the with phrase. Put your finger on the noun in that with phrase (*legs*) and ask students to put their finger on the noun that is not the subject and is in their with phrase.
17. Take the longest pink strip and ask students to write a '**that clause**' on the strip, and the '**that clause**' will tell us more about the noun.

    *Fabulous cheetahs with long <u>legs</u> **that move quickly** speed across the grasslands.*

18. Put the other long pick strips (30 cm x 4 cm) under the that clause you have on display and ask students to offer more 'that clauses' which can be added to describe legs.

    *with long **legs** that move quickly*

    that become a blur

    that touch the ground slightly

    that seem unreal

19. Students now write their own 'that clauses'.
20. Point to the 'that clause' (*that move quickly*) and ask what kind of clause it is? What is its function? What does this clause do? Elicit the statement that *that move quickly* describes the legs and is therefore a **describing clause**. Then ask for the proper name of a describing clause: **adjectival clause**.
21. Ask students to read their now very expanded noun groups:

    Fabulous cheetahs with long legs that move quickly

22. Question selected students about which noun is the main noun; what other nouns are there; what are they; how many adjectives are there; what are they; what is your adjectival phrase; what is your *that clause*?

    Note:
    Students have the opportunity to practise using a lot of metalanguage while using their own sentences or noun groups.

23. Ask your students to look at the display. Point to each of the adjectival clauses listed in the display (item 18). Underline the verbs in each clause, then ask students to tell you what the difference is between a clause and a phrase? What does a clause have that a phrase does not have? What must a clause always have? Run your finger down the line of verbs and ask what part of speech is each of those underlined words. The students will tell you that the words are **verbs**. They realise that *a clause always has a verb*, and the clause is different from a phrase because the phrase does not have a verb.

with long legs that <u>move</u> quickly

   that <u>become</u> a blur

   that <u>touch</u> the ground slightly

   that <u>seem</u> unreal

24. Make a space after the adjectival clause and ask students to look at the two blue strips, one for a phrase and the other for a clause.

25. Add a simile, as a *like* phrase (or an as *if clause*) to tell us how those legs moved so quickly.

   Fabulous cheetahs with long legs that move quickly
   like blurred wings...

   Fabulous cheetahs with long legs that move quickly
   as if they <u>were</u> blurred wings...

26. Students to add their own simile to their very expanded noun group.

27. Select students to read their very very expanded noun groups.

28. Quickly revise their understanding of the verb being in a clause. And talk also about simile, and how it tells us HOW something happens.

29. Ask six students to stand at the front of the room and bring one part of their sentence. You select the students and ask each to bring one of the following: original **noun group** (*fabulous cheetahs*), **adjectival phrase, adjectival clause, simile, verb, prepositional phrase**.

30. Ask students to read their part, and you will be given a sentence something like the following:

> *Cheeky monkeys with giant fins that have matted fur like shiny scales fly under the ground.*

Note:

Every student will want to be part of doing this little activity, and you can reinforce the metalanguage by asking students to bring out the required example (as in 29, above).

Ask students if they know a writer who mixes up phrases and clause like this? Dr Seuss. Point out that students now have three different ways to describe a noun and ask if writers use all three at the same time. Students will tell you that writers can select what to write.

What you are teaching your students is one of the many ways to make choices in writing to develop description and personal style. The *Australian Curriculum: English* requires students to be able to make choices in their writing, choices in vocabulary selection and use, phrases and clauses, and sentence variety.

You can teach this lesson in parts, giving your students opportunities to use their new knowledge and skill in daily writing activities. I would add in the new lesson every few days or a week between each. There is no need to rush this work and this long lesson incorporates more than 20% of primary school grammar. You have six years of primary school to teach grammar, and most students need practice, time, training and encouragement to use this knowledge in their writing.

Lesson 1: items 1 to 15

Lesson 2: (a) as in Lesson 1, but teach **adjectival clause** rather than adjectival phrase; *Fabulous cheetahs **that have long legs***

(b) items 16 to 23 (both phrase and clause)

Lesson 3: items 1 to 23

Lesson 4: items 1 to 30

EXPECTATIONS AND CONVENTIONS

There is continued debate about the value of using, let alone teaching the rules. But it is safer for writers to believe they are writing standard written English for an international audience. At the same time, an English program that focuses solely upon these conventions is unbalanced at best. Train students of writing to locate errors for themselves once you have shown the rule. Inability to see their problems as they edit their own writing may indicate lack of knowledge. See Campbell and Ryles (2018) for more information and approaches to assisting students.

Subject-verb agreement

There are three sets of rules.

Rule 1: **A singular subject takes a singular verb; a plural subject takes a plural verb.**

Example: *A cat drinks milk.* *Cats drink milk.*

The cat is purring. *The cats are purring.*

Some young children want to know why these rules are in place, and the only answer is "because that is how the language developed; and to have two ways of distinguishing singular and plural number". Troubles begin with the following instances:

a. **Collective noun**

   *The team **is** doing a great job.*

   (*The team **are** doing;* in US English)

b. **Everyone, everybody, anybody, anyone, none, no one:** always singular.

   But use of inclusive language allows the plural pronoun*.

   *Everybody **loves** their* pets.*

c. **Each, every, one**: always singular.

   Each tries to give their* gifts away.

d. **Number**: the hard rule is always singular.

   *The number **is** immaterial.*

e. **Some:** always plural.

   *Some (birds) **are** singing.*

f. **Majority/minority**: always plural.

   *The minority **are** sometimes right, as **are** the majority.*

g. **Any**: singular or plural verb, depending on the number in the group to which any refers:

   Because any may play, she is welcome.

   Because any may play, they are welcome.

   ***Any person is** welcome; any **ideas are** welcome.*

h. **None**: is singular, but increasingly used as a plural

   None is coming.

   (*None are coming* acceptable, but *No one is coming.*)

i. **Agenda**: is singular and takes a singular verb. (Agendas is the plural noun and takes the plural verb.)

j. **Correlatives**: *Either ... or; Neither ... nor*: Depends on the number of the second noun.

> Either that chicken or those **ducks** are to go.

> Neither those chickens nor that **goose** is to go.

k. **Summation nouns** such as scissors, binoculars, glasses: plural.

> These scissors **are** very sharp.

l. **Aggregate nouns** such as *media, data, news*: may be either singular or plural.

Use plural verb if data or media seems to be more than one.

(USA: *data* takes plural; in Australia, *data* is singular. *News* is singular.)

Rule 2: Agreement when there is more than one subject.

Type 1: (a) The **train** and the **bus** are coming.

(b) A knife and fork is used for eating steak.

How many items are involved in the actual subject? Train and bus are two different forms of transport, so the plural is needed. In (b) knife and fork are one set of cutlery items; therefore singular.

Type 2: Number of the second subject determines number of the verb.

(c) Only one or two rooms are available.

(d) Several small drinks or **one large drink** is enough.

Type 3: (e) The **children**, not the teacher, are responsible for their books.

(f) **One** of the parents is coming.

The writer asks: who is responsible? Who is coming? (i.e. test with the verb.)

Rule 3: **When subject and verb are separated by other information in the clause.**

Fabulous <u>cheetahs</u> with long legs
that move quickly <u>speed</u> *across the grasslands.*

The difficulty for many students is finding the verb. The subject is usually at the beginning of the sentence, so ask the question: *Fabulous cheetahs do what?*

Agreement of noun and pronoun

The general rule or principle is that the pronoun must agree with its referent noun in person, gender and number. Avoid most problems and write in plurals as often as you can.

In modern inclusive English, it is now permitted to use the plural pronoun *their* in order to refer to a singular noun that is not specific. For example, *a teacher should be aware of their responsibilities*. But *teachers* does the job better.

Preposition at the end of the sentence

This is a rule about which some grammar people like to expound. In reality, few serious writers are concerned about the position of the preposition. Clarity and message are the considerations.

David Crystal (1984) offers this gem to explain that clarity is the key to placing the preposition. *What are you going to cut down on?*

That is a situation I won't put up with. The often-quoted Churchill putdown about the rule: *That is a situation up with which I will not put.*

Fowler stated many years ago (1933) that if the final preposition is 'sounding comfortable', leave it there. Burchfield (1981) offers this delightful anecdote to show the robust nature of the preposition in living English. A little girl complains to her mother who has brought the wrong storybook for the bedtime reading session:

What did you bring that book I don't want read to out of up for?

Split infinitive

The term refers to placing an adverb or adjunct (*constantly* in the following examples) between the '*to*' and its verb. The infinitive form of the verb is signified by the use of to with the verb: *to strive, to seek, to find* and *not to yield*. (Tennyson's *Ulysses*)

> *The children wanted **to constantly play** marbles.*

The sentence could be stated as:

> *The children wanted to play marbles constantly.*
>
> or *The children constantly wanted to play marbles.*

The meaning shifts as the adverb (functioning as an adjunct) is shifted. The generally accepted principle is to avoid splitting the infinitive unless its placement in the middle 'sounds comfortable.'

Between you and me

Between you and me is grammatically correct, and should be used in formal English, both written and spoken. Reason: the pronoun case after a preposition is objective, so ▶ *between you and me*.

Between you and I is very widely used in spoken English in general conversation.

I/me

Pronouns in English are inflected to show whether they are subjective (*I*) or objective (*me*) or possessive (*my*) case.

> *I like to play football with my friends.*
>
> *My friends like to play football with me.*

me is correctly used as the object (objective case) of a verb or preposition.

It's I/me

Who is there? ***It's I*** is correct; grammatically because the being verb *is* does not take objective case. General usage breaks the grammatical rule, and the much more widely accepted and used expression is '***It's me***'.

Could have/could of

Could have is correct. *Could* is a modal verb and functions with the following verbs as part of the verb group. (Also applies to *would have, should have, must have* and *will have.*)

Different to/from/than

Use *different from* in all instances. NEVER use *different than*.

Different from avoids any problems.

Different to is used when two comparisons are contextually connected

> *The music of Spain is **different to** the tunes in Moldova.*

Try to/and

Try to every time, especially in formal written and spoken language. (*Try and* is acceptable in the context of informal uses of language.)

Kind/sort/type

When any of these words are used, all contingent words must keep the same number.

> *This kind of music is wonderful.*
>
> *These types of rhythms are catchy.*

Its/it's

It's always means *it is*.

Its is a possessive pronoun, and possessive pronouns do not have an apostrophe (except for *one's*).

Only

Place the adverb (or adjunct) *only* as near as possible to the word that it modifies.

>I wanted *only* to know the name.
>
>*Only* I wanted to know the name.
>
>I wanted to know *only* the name.
>
>I wanted to know the name *only*.

However

However is a word that is overused these days when *but* will do just as well.

However functions in two ways:

1. *However* used as a strong contrasting link between two ideas:

The food looked insignificant; however, it was incredibly delicious.

Hint: When *however* is used as a contrastive, there is an item of punctuation before and after.

2. *However* used as a subordinating conjunction:

However insignificant the food was, it was wonderfully scrumptious.

And/but/or at the beginning of a sentence

Use sparingly. Writers can choose to use these coordinating conjunctions at the sentence beginning for effect; and use them sparingly in order to get the effect.

Because at the beginning of a sentence

Use sparingly. Writers can choose to use these coordinating conjunctions at the sentence beginning for effect; and use sparingly in order to get the effect.

Dangling participle*/hanging phrases*

(See also incomplete clauses and noun groups)

> ***Waiting on the footpath***, *a car smashed into a post near me.*

This example shows the classic misplaced phrase, misplaced incomplete clause, or hanging phrase, also known as a dangling participle.

The participial phrase or incomplete clause can be rewritten as a complete clause:

> *As I was waiting on the footpath, a car smashed into a post near me.*

Solve this one:

> *Running along the old tracks, the children had a great time going to the museum on the train.*

Myself and reflexive forms of pronouns (see pronouns)

The reflexive form of the pronoun should be used sparingly and appropriately.

Reflexive pronouns refer back (reflect back) to an earlier pronoun:

> *She told me about it herself.*

Reflexive pronouns are sometimes used for emphasis.

> *I told him myself, just yesterday.*

> *They rebuilt the village themselves.*

> *He poached the eggs himself.*

But reflexive pronouns are **NOT to be used in the objective case.**

He gave it to myself is not correct. ▶ *He gave it to me is correct.*

Who/whom/whose/which/that (relative pronouns)

These words are relative pronouns and relate to nouns or pronouns in front of them in the sentence. Relative pronouns are used as special forms of conjunctions to join a dependent adjectival clause to the related noun or pronoun.

Who (subjective case), *whom* (objective case), and *whose* (possessive case) are also inflected for case (shown in brackets).

Sentence fragments

A sentence begins with a capital letter and ends with a full stop or other accepted boundary marker. But a sentence also must have a verb and include all connected ideas and clauses. For example:

> *The whole place was jumping.* **Which said a lot for the band playing its first gig.**

The full stop after 'jumping' should be replaced with a comma, and the capital W with a lower case w.

Note:

As a general principle, never use fragments or run-on sentences in formal writing.

Run-on sentences

The run-on sentence occurs when the writer does not use an appropriate boundary marker between clauses. This causes the reader a problem because readers use the convention of sentences unconsciously when reading. They become confused because the writer's mistakes obscure the meaning of the text.

Don't use run-on sentences they are too hard to read they interfere with my automatic application of knowledge about the structure and look of written English.

Maintain verb tense

Recounts of events are usually spoken and written in the simple past tense.

*We **drove** to the city and **had** a great time.*

Reports about phenomena are written about in the present tense.

*Water **finds** its own level.*

(also known as the timeless present tense)

Redundancy

Saying the same thing twice.

Amy is progressing well and making good progress.

I myself was the only one to think of the answer.

The grammar check on Microsoft Word

Give up. If your sentence construction is outside the few examples provided in Microsoft Word grammar-check, then you will be asked to re-write. Cleft and pseudo-cleft sentences and passive voice have been edited out, seemingly in an attempt to provide a program for plain English. The reality is that the limitations of grammar-check are so unlimited as to make the software a hazard for writers and learning writers. That is, obeying every direction from grammar-check and similar programs is an invitation to boring sameness in writing. However, artificial intelligence (AI) applied to such programs in the future will assist good writing.

REFERENCES

Bean-Folkes, J. & Campbell, R. (2019). *Writing and Reading: A Book of Language Lessons.* Dubuque, Iowa: Kendall Hunt.

Berenstain, S. (1972). *Bears in the Night.* London: Random House.

Campbell, R. & Ryles, G. (2018) 2nd ed. *Teaching English Grammar.* Sydney: Pearson.

Campbell, R. (1996). *Teaching grammar.* PhD Thesis. University of Queensland.

Crystal, D. (1984). *Who cares about English Usage?* Harmondsworth, England: Penguin.

Fowler, H. W. (1965). *A dictionary of modern English usage.* 2nd edn. revised by E. Gowers. Oxford: Oxford University Press.

Gerot, L. & Wignell, P. (1994). *Making sense of functional grammar.* Sydney: Antipodean.

Halliday, M. A. K. (1985). *An introduction to functional grammar.* London: Edward Arnold.

Halliday, M. A. K. (1985). *Spoken and written language.* Geelong, Vic: Deakin University Press.

Halliday, M. A. K. (2004). *An introduction to functional grammar.* (3rd ed). London: Hodder Arnold.

Harris, M. (1986). *Teaching one-to-one: The writing conference.* Washington, D.C.: National Council of Teachers of English.

Hudson, R. (1992). *Teaching grammar: A guide for the national curriculum.* Oxford: Basil Blackwell.

Lewis, C. S. (1983). *The Lion, the Witch and the Wardrobe.* Collins.

Martin, B. (1967). *Brown Bear Brown Bear.* New York: Holt, Rinehart & Winston.

McCracken, R. A. and McCracken, M. J. (1986). *Stories, songs and poetry to teach reading and writing: Literacy through language.* Chicago: American Library Association.

Nash, W. (1986). *English usage: A guide to first principles.* London: Routledge and Kegan Paul.

Peters, P. (ed.) (1990). *The Macquarie file writers guide.* Brisbane: Jacaranda Press.

Rubinstein, G. (1988). *Answers to Brut.* Omnibus Books.

Rubinstein, G. (1986). *Space Demons.* Omnibus Books.

Strunk, W. & White, E. B. (1979). *The elements of style.* 3rd ed. NY: Macmillian.

Strunk, W. & White, E. B. (2000). *The elements of style.* 4th ed. NY: Longman.

Style manual for authors, editors and printers (2002: 6th ed.) Brisbane: Wiley (for the Australian Government).

Sutton, E. (1973). *My cat likes to hide in boxes.* (Illus. by Lynley Dodd.) London: Hamilton.

The Australian Concise Oxford English Dictionary (2004: 4th ed.) Melbourne: OUP.

Tompkins G., Campbell, R., Green, D. & Smith, C. (2015). *Literacy for the 21st Century.* 2nd Australian edition. Sydney: Pearson Education Australia.

Tompkins G., Smith, C., Campbell, R. & Green, D. (2019). *Literacy for the 21st Century.* 3rd Australian edition. Sydney: Pearson Education Australia.

Ur, P. (1988). *Grammar practice activities: A practical guide for teachers.* Cambridge: Cambridge University Press.

INDEX

a, an (indefinite article) 179
abbreviation 118–119
abstract noun 138
active voice 146–147
adjective 155–160
adjectival clause 169
adjectival phrase 121–122
adverb 161–166
adverbial clause 124–125
adverbial phrase 121, 177
ampersand 111
antonyms 163
apostrophe
   of omission 143
   of possession 141–143
article 179–180
asterisk 111

bibliography 40
brackets 41

capital letters 113
case (pronouns) 167–169
circumstance 177
clause 123–134
closed class words
   conjunction 135
   prepositions 175
   pronouns 167
collective noun 54, 138
colon 41
comma 131–134
comment 117–118, 133
common noun 55, 137
comparatives 156–157
complete clause 124, 129

complex sentence 98
conjunction 135–136
continuous tense 107
contraction
   with apostrophe 33, 143
   without apostrophe 85
coordinating conjunction 95, 123–124, 135
correlative conjunction 136

dangling modifier 129–130
dash 42
definite article 179
demonstratives 181
dependent clause 124–128
direct object 148
direct speech 44, 134

ellipsis 112
embedding 169
exclamation mark 91

full stop 117–119
future tense 107

gender
   inclusive 55, 170
   nouns 138
   pronouns 167–170
gerund 34

hanging particle 127, 129–130
hanging phrase 196
hatch 111
hyphen 42–43

idiom 52–53
imperative mood 147–148
incomplete (non-finite) clause 128–130
indefinite article 179–180
indefinite pronoun 55, 168
independent clause 123–128, 131–134
indicative mood 147–148
indirect object 148
indirect speech 45
infinitive 128, 145–146, 193
inflection of adjectives 156
interrogative question 56, 147
intransitive verb 148–149
irregular verb 149
italics 111

learning log 49, 102
loose sentence 132

metaphor 70, 160
modal auxiliary 148
modifiers 161
mood 147–148

neuter gender 168
non-sexist language 55
noun 137–144
noun phrase 121

object 148
open punctuation 77, 81, 85

paragraph 16–17
parenthesis 41
participle 127–129, 146–147, 149, 151, 196
passive voice 146–147, 198
past tense 43, 107, 145–146, 149
periodic sentence 127
phrase 121–122
plurals 55, 141
positive degree 156
possessive apostrophe 141–142
possessive pronoun 143, 195
predicate 117–118, 146, 185
preposition 177, 192–193
prepositional phrase 122, 177–178, 187
present participle 32, 128, 149
present tense 107, 198,
pronoun 167–174
proper noun 53, 137
punctuation 12, 41, 90, 118, 131, 141

question mark 90
quotation marks 90, 105

references 39, 40
reflexive pronouns 196–197
relative pronoun 168–169, 180, 197

semicolon 41
sentence 113–120
simile 160, 187
singular 54–55, 65, 142, 189–191
solidus 111
speech marks 90, 105
split infinitive 193
subject 63–64, 117–118, 133–134, 146, 189–192
subject-verb agreement 189–192
subjunctive 147–148
subordinating conjunction 124, 195
superlative degree 197

tense 43, 107, 145–146, 151, 198
the (definite article) 179
titles 85
topic 28, 117–118, 133
transitive verb 148–149

verb 145–154
voice 146–147

Index **203**

www.ingramcontent.com/pod-product-compliance
Lightning Source LLC
Chambersburg PA
CBHW071612080526
44588CB00010B/1105